The
Artful
Vegetarian

The
Artful
Vegetarian

by Karen Meyer

GREENHOUSE PUBLICATIONS

First published in 1988 by
Greenhouse Publications Pty Ltd
385 Bridge Road
Richmond   Victoria   3121

© Karen Meyer, 1988

Cover and book design by Leonie Stott
Cover photograph by Peter Williams, courtesy of Auschromes
Illustrated by Leon Meyer

Typeset in 10½/11pt Korinna by
Meredith Typesetting, Richmond
Printed in Australia by
Brown Prior Anderson

National Library of Australia
Cataloguing-in-Publication data:

  Meyer, Karen.
    The artful vegetarian.
    Includes index.
    ISBN 0 86436 111 4.
    1. Vegetarian cookery.
    I. Title.
641.5'636

DEDICATION

In recognition of her help, encouragement and support over the years, this book is dedicated to my mother with thanks.

ACKNOWLEDGEMENTS

A special thank you to Leon for the great sketches and his help and advice on the book. To Sandie and Jan for being there, to my 1987 Year 12 Brighton Tech students for all the recipe testing, and to Marli for her help with testing, trying and commenting on many of the recipes.

Contents

Introduction

For most of us, food plays a significant and enjoyable part in our lives. Nothing can quite beat the smell of fresh bread baking, or the sight of the season's first cherries arriving in the shops.

It is a simple fact that what we eat, together with how much rest and exercise we get, determines how we are as people. Our happiness comes from within, so we should give ourselves the best.

Eating wisely is a treat for our bodies and it can be throughly enjoyable. We need to eat plenty of fresh fruits and vegetables, wholegrains and low-fat protein foods. We should choose processed foods with care, since they are often high in fats, sugars and preservatives.

In writing *The Artful Vegetarian*, I hope to provide recipes which make good food beautiful to look at, delicious to eat and highly nutritious. Remember it is best to eat foods in their natural state as far as possible.

I firmly believe that our children need to be taught about good food and diet. They also need to be taught to discriminate when choosing treats from the vast array of snack foods and take-aways on offer. I would really love to see the 'You can say "No"' campaign extended to other areas such as junk food, smoking and drugs.

Parents have control over the diets of younger children and at this time it is important to see that the children develop a good eating pattern. As they grow older they need to learn what are appropriate amounts of food for them to eat with regard to their growth and activity levels and we must help them gain the confidence to make decisions themselves. As adults we should establish an acceptable body weight for ourselves and then strive to maintain that weight as energetic and enthusiastic individuals.

Eat wisely, eat well!

About the recipes

The recipes are written so that variations can be made depending on your needs or what foods you have available. For example, tofu, ricotta cheese, and cottage cheese are interchangeable in most recipes. Tofu does not need much cooking time, so allow for this.

There are a variety of cookies etc. that do not use wheat flour, to allow for people with wheat allergies.

The use of oil has been kept to an absolute minimum, and vegetable salt has been suggested a few times where tamari would not be suitable.

Cooking times are approximate and depend on the type of container the food is cooked in and the type of oven used. The use of a food processor or blender is suggested often as they are wonderful pieces of equipment to have for vegetarian cooking. At the end of some recipes suggestions are made as to what to serve with the food. These take into consideration the total food value of the meal as well as the texture and overall appearance and appeal.

The rest is up to you and your imagination. Happy cooking!

Dips and starters

AVOCADO AND COCONUT ICE

Using creamy smooth coconut milk with avocado this makes a delicious hot day treat when served as an entree.

3 small very soft avocadoes

$^1/_2$ cup coconut cream

1 cup milk or soy milk

juice of a lemon

few drops coconut essence

shredded coconut

Place the avocado flesh, coconut cream, milk, lemon juice and essence in a food processor and blend until smooth. Freeze until nearly firm. Blend again until smooth and refreeze. Let it stand out of freezer for 15 minutes before serving in small scoops with shredded coconut and a few orange segments or avocado slices alongside.

AVOCADO DIP DELIGHT

Just perfect as a dip or spread for dinner parties or dolloped over salads or hot steamed vegetables.

1 large ripe avocado
2 tomatoes, chopped and well drained
2 cloves garlic, crushed
juice of a lemon
½ teaspoon vegetable salt
4 spring onions, finely sliced

Combine the avocado, tomatoes, garlic, lemon juice and salt in a food processor and blend until smooth. Stir in the spring onions and serve or refrigerate.

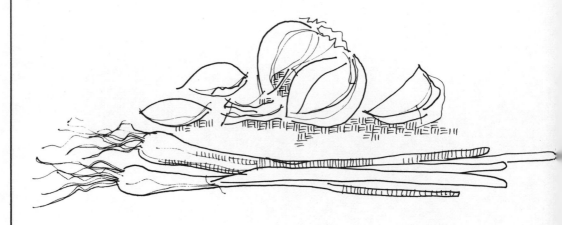

AVOCADO PEAR ENTREE

For a delicious and easy to prepare first course, serve avocadoes.
Choose just ripe avocadoes and allow one half per person.

½ cup slivered almonds
2 avocadoes
juice of a lemon, strained
1 green capsicum, thinly sliced and cut in 2-3 cm lengths
½ red capsicum, thinly sliced and cut in 2-3 cm lengths
6 spring onions, sliced on the diagonal in 2 cm lengths
8 black olives, stoned and sliced
1 tablespoon oil
1 tablespoon apple cider vinegar
black pepper
½ teaspoon vegetable salt (optional)
some watercress or fennel for decoration

Toast the almonds on a dry baking tray in a moderate oven until golden. Cut the avocadoes in half lengthways and remove the stone. Peel carefully and brush completely with lemon juice. Place the avocadoes cut side down on serving plates. Drop the chopped green and red capsicums and spring onions into a little boiling water, cook for 1 minute only, then drain and rinse well with cold water. Drain again. To make the dressing combine the olives, oil, vinegar, pepper and vegetable salt. Toss well. Add the capsicums and spring onions to the dressing. Spoon the dressing over the avocadoes leaving some on the top and the remainder around the sides. Sprinkle with the toasted slivered almonds and serve with a little watercress or fennel on the side.

BAKED AVOCADO MAGIC

Try these as an entree for an exciting surprise.

2 teaspoons oil
1 clove garlic, crushed
6 spring onions, finely sliced
¼ teaspoon tumeric
2 tomatoes, finely diced
¾ cup fresh wholemeal breadcrumbs
½ teaspoon tamari or vegetable salt
black pepper
2 avocadoes
juice of half a lemon
thin lemon wedges for serving
cornchips

Heat the oil in a frypan and lightly cook the garlic, spring onions and tumeric for 3-4 minutes. Add the tomatoes and stir for 2 minutes and then take off the heat and mix in the breadcrumbs, tamari, and pepper. Cut the avocadoes in half lengthwise and remove the stone. Brush with lemon juice. Pile the filling into the avocado hollows, place on a baking tray and bake in a moderate oven at 180°C for 10 minutes. Serve hot with the lemon wedges and corn chips.

MAGICAL AVOCADO AND FETTA DIP

Delectable and creamy, this is a winner. Serve with crunchy natural corn chips, or crisp vegetable pieces.

1 large ripe avocado
1/2 cup fetta cheese
3/4 cup ricotta, or creamy cottage cheese
1 tablespoon natural yoghurt
juice of a lemon
1/4 teaspoon curry powder
1/4 teaspoon tumeric
1/4 teaspoon vegetable salt
black pepper

Combine all ingredients together in a blender or food processor and blend until smooth. Chill until needed.

MUSHROOM AND ALMOND PATE

A well seasoned pâté, this is perfect for occasions that call for a tasty and elegant appetiser. Serve with corn chips or sesame biscuits, or slice and present on a plate with crusty bread.

1 cup (100 g) slivered almonds
2 teaspoons oil
1 small onion, chopped
2 cloves crushed garlic
500 g sliced mushrooms
1/4 teaspoon dried thyme, or 1/2 teaspoon fresh thyme
1 teaspoon tamari
black pepper
1-2 tablespoons extra oil or soy milk

Toast the almonds on a dry baking tray in a moderate oven for 6-8 minutes until golden. Heat the oil and fry the onion and garlic for 3-4 minutes. Add the mushrooms and cook for a further 5 minutes, stirring often. Stir in the thyme, tamari and pepper. Blend the almonds in a food processor, slowly adding the oil or soy milk until it is creamy. Add the mushroom mixture and continue to blend until smooth. Pack into a lightly oiled pâté dish and bake in a moderate oven for 15-20 minutes or until firm. Cool and serve with a sprig of fresh herbs or fennel on the side.

MUSHROOM AND CARROT PATE

This is rather different, and extremely tasty. Try it for lunch or a special dinner.

2 onions, finely chopped
2 cloves garlic, crushed
½ tablespoon oil
500 g mushrooms, minced in a food processor
1 teaspoon tamari
black pepper
4 cups finely grated carrots
1 cup ground almonds or cashews
½ cup finely chopped parsley
½ teaspoon dried thyme
¼ teaspoon each dried oregano, celery seed and allspice
½ teaspoon mustard mixed with a little water
squeeze of lemon juice
1 cup well mashed tofu, ricotta or cottage cheese

Lightly fry the onions and garlic in oil over a moderate heat until clear. Add the mushrooms and cook while stirring until the liquid has evaporated. Season with tamari and pepper, then blend in a food processor until smooth. Combine with all of the remaining ingredients, mixing well. Pile the mixture into a well oiled loaf pan, cover with foil and place in a baking dish. Half fill the baking dish with cold water. Bake in a moderate oven for 30 to 40 minutes or until dry and firm to the touch. Allow to chill completely before serving. Turn out onto a serving plate and garnish with very thin slices of cucumber. Serve with Herb Sauce and fresh wholemeal or rye bread.

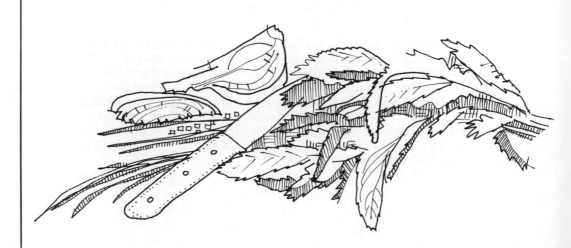

RATATOUILLE APPETISERS

Little pastry triangles filled with a ratatouille mixture make a tasty and interesting change for an appetiser.

PASTRY

1 ½ cups each of plain wholemeal flour and unbleached white flour

½ cup margarine or butter

½ cup or more of warm water to mix

FILLING

1 tablespoon oil or water

2 cloves crushed garlic

2 onions, finely chopped

2 cups button mushrooms, finely sliced

6 small zucchini, sliced

3 tomatoes, diced

2 small capsicum, diced

½ cup black olives, chopped

2 teaspoons dried tomato flakes

1 teaspoon tamari

black pepper

To make the filling, heat oil or water and gently cook onion and garlic until soft. Stir in mushrooms, zucchini, tomatoes and capsicum and cook for 3 minutes. Stir in remaining ingredients and take mixture off the heat.

To make the pastry, sift the flours together, rub in the butter or margarine until it resembles breadcrumbs, add warm water to make a soft dough and knead a little on a lightly floured bench. Roll pastry out to ½ cm thick, cut into diamonds 8 cm wide by 15 cm long, then cut each diamond across to make 2 triangles. Fold up the sides of each triangle about 1 cm deep crimping corners together. Place the pastry cases on a baking tray and fill with vegetable mixture. Bake in a 200°C oven for 15-20 minutes until pastry is browned. Serve warm. Makes about 25-30 appetisers.

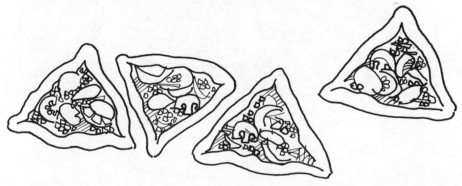

DIPS AND STARTERS

SPICY TOFU PATE

This pâté is both flavoursome and quick to make, but needs to be well chilled before using. It can be refrigerated for up to a week.

2 long thin carrots
1 long thin zucchini or leek
2 cups tofu
½ cup wholemeal flour or soy flour
3 teaspoons tamari
1 teaspoon oregano
½ teaspoon marjoram or thyme
¼ teaspoon dill
¼ teaspoon celery seed (optional)
2 teaspoons prepared mustard
1 clove of garlic

Put the carrots on to steam for 5 minutes, add the zucchini, steam for another 5 minutes and then cool. Mash the tofu in a large bowl. Add all of the remaining ingredients and mix well with your hands. Put half of this mixture into a lightly oiled loaf tin. Lie the zucchini along the centre, and the carrots along either side of the zucchini. Cover with the remaining mixture, then with foil. Place in a baking dish of water and bake in a moderate oven for 25-35 minutes. Cool before removing and serve with toasted rye fingers.

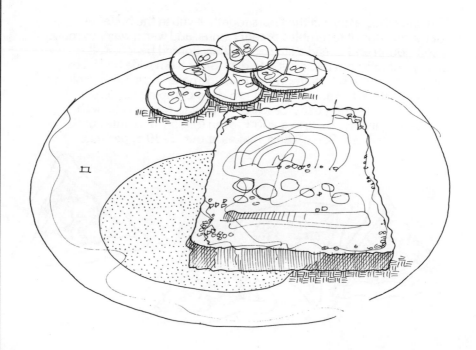

SUNSHINE BALL

This recipe makes an interesting change from a dip.

2 tablespoons chopped dates

1 tablespoon freshly squeezed orange juice

250 g ricotta cheese, low fat cottage cheese or well
mashed tofu

2 tablespoons chopped walnuts

1 tablespoon chopped raisins

1 teaspoon each chopped parsley and chives

2 tablespoons extra chopped mixed nuts

Soak the dates in the orange juice for 2 hours. Mash the dates into
the cheese or tofu, with the nuts, raisins, parsley and chives. Shape
this mixture into a ball. Cover with the extra nuts. Wrap and chill
until needed. Serve in lettuce leaves as a snack with sliced apple,
celery curls and wholemeal crispbread.

TERRINE OF VEGETABLES WITH FRESH TOMATO SAUCE

Delectably different and a winner as a low fat starter.

$^1/_2$ bunch of asparagus, trimmed
1 cup fresh peas
2 whole zucchini
2 cups cauliflower pieces
2 cups broccoli pieces
1 cup mashed tofu
1 cup cooked brown rice
juice of a lemon
a little grated nutmeg
a little vegetable salt or tamari
1 tablespoon tahini, if desired
2 tablespoons agar-agar powder
$^1/_2$ cup vegetable water
$^1/_2$ bunch spinach or silverbeet leaves, trimmed
Fresh Tomato Sauce
thinly sliced cucumber for serving

Lightly cook the asparagus, peas and zucchini in a little water until just tender, drain, cool and reserve the liquid. Steam the cauliflower and broccoli pieces, drain and cool. In a food processor or blender puree the cauliflower and broccoli with the tofu, rice, lemon juice, nutmeg, vegetable salt and tahini. Sprinkle the agar-agar over the reserved vegetable water, bring it to the boil and simmer until it dissolves.

Meanwhile, blanch the spinach leaves in boiling water for one minute, drain well and pat dry. Lightly oil a large terrine or loaf tin, line with the spinach leaves allowing plenty of overhang. Stir the dissolved agar-agar into the cauliflower mixture. Spread a layer of the cauliflower mix over the base of the dish. Arrange the asparagus across the dish, then layer more cauliflower mix, then the green peas, cauliflower mix, then the zucchini laying lengthwise and finish with cauliflower mix. Fold the overhanging spinach leaves over the terrine completely enclosing the contents. Cover with foil. Place in a baking dish half-filled with hot water and bake in a moderate oven for 40-45 minutes. Cool and refrigerate. To serve, cut terrine into thick slices and arrange on top of a pool of Fresh Tomato Sauce spread on plates. Decorate with cucumber slices.

Soups

AVOCADO AND ZUCCHINI SOUP

Perfectly simple, and particularly tasty.

500 g zucchini, sliced
4 cups water
2 large, very ripe avocadoes
3 tablespoons lemon juice
2 teaspoons tamari
1/2 cup natural yoghurt
3/4 teaspoon dried coriander
1/2 teaspoon brown sugar
pinch of tumeric
1 cup chopped and seeded tomatoes

Place the zucchini and water in a saucepan, bring to the boil and simmer for 10 minutes or until very soft. Remove the zucchini and reserve the liquid. Puree the zucchini with the peeled and stoned avocadoes in a food processor. Whisk this puree into the soup liquid along with the lemon juice, tamari, yoghurt, coriander, brown sugar and tumeric. Heat without boiling and serve in warmed soup bowls. Sprinkle with the chopped tomatoes and serve with triangles of wholemeal melba toast.

CREAMY ASPARAGUS SOUP

A dinner party delight when asparagus is in season.

1 tablespoon oil
2 onions, chopped
2 leeks, washed and chopped
2 sticks celery, sliced
2 bunches asparagus, trimmed and chopped
1 cup diced potato
4 cups water
1/2-1 teaspoon vegetable salt
1 cup soy milk (optional) or cow's milk
chopped parsley or snipped chives

Heat the oil in a large saucepan and lightly fry the onions and leeks for 5 minutes. Add the celery, asparagus, potato, water and vegetable salt. Bring to the boil and simmer 15 to 20 minutes until the vegetables are soft. Cool. Puree this in a food processor or blender until creamy. Add the milk and reheat gently. Sprinkle each bowl with the parsley or chives.

CREAMY SPINACH SOUP

Always a welcome and nourishing soup.

2 onions, chopped
1 clove of garlic
1 bunch spinach, well washed
2 potatoes, peeled and chopped
3 cups water
a little grated nutmeg
1/4 teaspoon dill seed
squeeze of lemon juice
1/2 teaspoon vegetable salt or tamari
black pepper
1 cup milk, soy milk or coconut cream

Cook the onions and garlic in a saucepan with a little oil or water for 5 minutes. Reserve a few spinach leaves for decorating the soup, then chop the remaining spinach leaves and stems. Return these to the saucepan and add the potatoes and the water. Bring to the boil and simmer for 10 minutes. Puree the soup in a food processor or blender, return it to the saucepan and stir in the nutmeg, dill, lemon, vegetable salt, pepper and milk. Bring soup back to simmering point and serve in warmed soup bowls. Garnish with the reserved spinach leaves cut into thin ribbons and serve with lightly toasted rice cakes or crackers.

DUET OF SOUPS

Unusual and very pretty to serve on special occasions.

CAULIFLOWER SOUP

½ cauliflower, in small sprigs

2 medium potatoes, peeled and chopped

2 cups water

½ teaspoon vegetable salt, if desired

½ cup milk or soy milk

pinch of grated nutmeg

black pepper

CARROT SOUP

2 medium carrots, peeled and grated

1 onion, chopped

½ cup fresh orange juice, strained

1½ cups water

½ teaspoon vegetable salt, if desired

½ cup milk or soy milk

black pepper

GARNISH

natural yoghurt

chives

Using separate saucepans, cook the cauliflower/potato and carrot/orange combination in the water for 12-15 minutes or until very soft. Add the remaining ingredients to each and puree or blend separately until creamy smooth. Return soup to individual saucepans. Heat through and thin with a little extra milk if needed. Pour each soup into a warm cup. Holding a cup in each hand, pour the soups simultaneously into each warmed bowl. Top each bowl with a dollop of natural yoghurt and snipped chives. Serves 4.

LIGHT 'N LOVELY GREEN SOUP

Packed with nutrients, this soup is a delightful start to a meal. If watercress is unavailable it can be omitted, but it adds a depth to the flavour, so search for it at your local market.

2 leeks, sliced
2 medium potatoes, chopped
2 zucchini, chopped
3 sticks of celery, sliced
3 cups cucumber pieces
1 cup parsley sprigs
½ cup fresh coriander
1 bunch of watercress, chopped
½-1 tablespoon tamari, or ½ teaspoon vegetable salt

Cook the leeks in just a little water in a large saucepan until the water evaporates and the leeks have started to soften. Add all of the remaining ingredients except the tamari. Add water to come half way up the vegetables and bring to the boil. Cover and simmer for 10 to 12 minutes or until the vegetables are tender. Cool a little then puree the mixture in a blender. Add the tamari or vegetable salt and some white pepper if desired. When reheating the soup, extra water or soy milk may be added to bring the soup to the right consistency. Serve the soup with a sprig of fresh herbs or snipped chives on top.

Children will enjoy the subtle flavour of this soup.

MISOSHIRU
– Clear Japanese Soup

A clear and tasty soup to stimulate the appetite. The shapes in which the vegetables are cut is a feature of this dish.

2 cups water
2 long thin carrots, thinly sliced on the diagonal
2 stalks of celery, thinly sliced on the diagonial
2 tablespoons light coloured miso
1 cup tofu pieces cut in 1 cm cubes
6 spring onions, thinly sliced on the diagonal
1-2 teaspoons tamari
2-3 cups extra water

Heat the water. Add the carrots and simmer 5 minutes. Add the celery and simmer a further 3 minutes. Dissolve the miso in a little of the hot liquid and add the remaining ingredients and extra water. Stir to blend. Bring to the boil and simmer 2-3 minutes, adding extra tamari if necessary. Serve at once.

MUSHROOM AND LENTIL SOUP

Certainly a filling soup

1 cup brown lentils, well washed
1 tablespoon oil
2 onions, chopped
1 clove garlic, crushed
2 cups sliced mushrooms
½ teaspoon ground ginger, or 1 teaspoon grated fresh root ginger
½ teaspoon dried coriander
3 cups water
½ cup fresh orange juice
2 teaspoons tamari
black pepper
2 tablespoons chopped parsley

Put the lentils in a saucepan, just cover with cold water, bring to the boil and simmer for 10 minutes letting some of the water evaporate. In another pan, heat the oil and cook the onions and garlic until clear. Add the mushrooms, ginger and coriander and cook, while stirring, for a further 3 minutes. Drain the lentils and add to the onion and mushroom mixture along with the water and orange juice. Bring to the boil, then simmer for 20-25 minutes until the lentils are soft. Add the tamari and pepper.

As this soup is a dull grey colour, serve it with plenty of parsley sprinkled on top and a colourful salad and vegetable dish.

MUSHROOM, LEEK AND POTATO SOUP

Always a delight.

1 tablespoon oil
1 clove garlic, crushed
2 onions, diced
2 leeks, chopped
500 g mushrooms, chopped
2 cups chopped potatoes
3 cups water
2 teaspoons white miso
2 teaspoons tamari
black pepper
3 extra mushrooms, thinly sliced
chives for garnish

Heat the oil in a large saucepan and lightly fry the garlic, onions and leeks for 5 minutes. Add the mushrooms and cook a further 3-4 minutes. Add the potatoes and water, bring to the boil, cover and simmer 10-15 minutes or until the potatoes are tender. Cool a little, then blend in a food processor with the white miso, tamari and black pepper until creamy. Reheat and serve with 3 thin mushroom slices in each bowl and a few snipped chives on top.
Yum!

PUMPKIN AND RED LENTIL SOUP

A simple soup to make, the red lentils in this provide extra flavour, colour and nourishment.

2 large onions, chopped
1 clove garlic, crushed, optional
4 cups chopped pumpkin
1 cup red lentils, washed and soaked 1 hour
1 teaspoon tumeric
½ teaspoon cumin
water to cover
1 tablespoon fresh chopped coriander, or 1 teaspoon dried coriander
2 teaspoons tamari
black pepper
1 cup tofu cut in small cubes
½ cup alfalfa sprouts

Simmer the onions and garlic in a little water until soft. Add the pumpkin, lentils, tumeric, cumin and water. Bring to the boil and simmer for 25-30 minutes stirring occasionally. Cool and blend with the coriander leaves in a blender until smooth. Add the tamari and pepper. Heat and serve with the tofu and sprouts scattered over the top.

THICK AND LIGHT VEGETABLE SOUP

Just perfect for a cold winter's day. The vegetables can be varied according to whatever is in season.

½ cup water
1 onion, chopped
1 leek, sliced
2 stalks celery, sliced
½ cup green peas
1 cup broccoli pieces
1 cup cauliflower pieces
½ cup carrot, diced
½ cup zucchini, diced
3 cups water, or more as needed
1 full tablespoon of light coloured miso
1 cup of tofu cubes
2 teaspoons of tamari
½ cup chopped parsley

Put the ½ cup of water, onion and leeks into a large saucepan. Simmer for 2 to 3 minutes, or until the water evaporates. Add the remaining vegetables and water, bring to the boil, and simmer until tender, about 10 to 15 minutes. Combine the miso with a little of the hot soup liquid, and mix until smooth. Return this to the soup along with the tofu cubes and tamari. Reheat and serve sprinkled with the parsley.

This is a balanced meal on its own when served with whole wheat or rye bread.

THICK CORN AND PUMPKIN SOUP

This hearty and warming soup from Sandie, is welcome on a wintery day.

2 cups sweet corn kernels, fresh if possible
4 cups roughly chopped pumpkin, include the skin if it is a good dark blue colour
1 cup green split peas
3-4 cups water
a little grated nutmeg
a little vegetable salt or tamari
chives or parsley for serving

Reserve ½ a cup of corn kernels for decoration. Place the vegetables, split peas and water into a large saucepan. Bring to the boil and simmer for 30-40 minutes or until the split peas are soft. Stir in the nutmeg, vegetable salt or tamari. Blend or puree the soup until it is thick and creamy. Serve with a few corn kernels in the centre of each bowl and a few snipped chives or parsley sprigs scattered on top. Fresh or toasted black rye bread can be served to complete a perfect and filling lunch.

TOMATO AND ORANGE SOUP

What a taste sensation!

2 onions, finely chopped
8-10 ripe tomatoes, chopped
2 cups chopped carrots
1 teaspoon tomato flakes
4 cups water
piece of lemon rind
bay leaf
1 cup fresh orange juice
1 teaspoon honey
½ teaspoon vegetable salt or 2 teaspoons tamari

Put the onions in a saucepan with a little cold water, bring to the boil and simmer until the water evaporates and the onions are clear. Add the tomatoes, carrots, tomato flakes, water, lemon rind and bay leaf. Bring to the boil and simmer for 10 minutes. Remove the bay leaf and lemon rind. Cool, then puree in a food processor until smooth. Add the orange juice, honey and vegetable salt or tamari. Reheat and serve.

Cold vegetable dishes and salads

AVOCADO AND ALMOND SALAD

1/2 cup slivered almonds

1 radichion or mignonette lettuce

2 just ripe avocadoes

1/2 tablespoon oil

juice of half a lemon

1/4 teaspoon vegetable salt

pinch of dry mustard

black pepper

6 spring onions, cut in 3 cm lengths

basil leaves

Toast the almonds on a dry baking tray in the oven until golden. Lie the lettuce leaves on a serving plate. Cut the avocadoes in half, peel and slice then place them over the lettuce. Toss together the oil, lemon juice, salt, mustard and pepper and sprinkle over the avocado. Scatter the spring onions and basil leaves on top and then the toasted slivered almonds. Serve.

BROCCOLI, LEEK AND WALNUT SALAD

1 leek, thinly sliced on the diagonal (1 cm)
2 cups broccoli flowers
2 thin zucchini, sliced on the diagonal
2 cups finely shredded red cabbage
1 cup toasted walnuts
½ tablespoon oil
juice of ½ a lemon
2 teaspoons cider vinegar
¼ teaspoon vegetable salt
ground black peppercorns

Steam the leeks, broccoli and zucchini until just tender but still brightly coloured. Cool. Combine with the red cabbage and walnuts. Mix together the oil, lemon juice, vinegar, salt and pepper. Toss the mixture through the salad and serve.

BUTTERNUT PUMPKIN AND WALNUT SALAD

½ tablespoon oil
juice of a lemon
1 clove of garlic
1 teaspoon tamari or ½ teaspoon vegetable salt
500 g butternut pumpkin, thinly sliced
250 g snow peas
3 zucchini, thinly sliced
1 tablespoon water
½ cup walnuts

Heat the oil, lemon juice, garlic and tamari in a frypan, add the pumpkin slices and simmer 5 minutes. Add the snow peas, zucchini and water and cook a further 2-3 minutes. Stir in the walnuts and serve.

CELERY AND SESAME SALAD

1 1/2 cups sliced celery

1/2 cup chopped green capsicum

1 cucumber, sliced in half rings

1/2 cup sliced radishes

4 tomatoes, cut in wedges

6 spring onions, sliced

1 tablespoon each toasted sesame seeds and raisins

DRESSING

2 tablespoons cold pressed oil

1 tablespoon cider vinegar

juice of 1/2 a lemon

1/2 teaspoon mustard

1/2 teaspoon vegetable salt

1/2 tablespoon chopped parsley

a little chopped mint

Combine all the vegetable salad ingredients together and add the sesame seeds and raisins. Mix all the dressing ingredients together. Pour over the salad and toss well.

COLD NOODLES WITH SPINACH AND MUSHROOMS

A surprisingly different salad for those hot summer days.

500 g thin wholemeal noodles

2 cups young spinach leaves

2 cups thinly sliced button mushrooms

6 spring onions, thinly sliced on the diagonal

2 teaspoons tamari

1 teaspoon finely grated fresh ginger

grated rind from 1/2 a lemon

1 tablespoon sunflower seeds toasted until golden

alfalfa sprouts for decoration

Cook the noodles in plenty of boiling water with a dash of oil in it to prevent the noodles sticking. Meanwhile, cook the spinach, mushrooms and spring onions in just a little boiling water for 2 to 3 minutes. Drain and chill quickly. Drain the noodles and cool. Combine the noodles with the chilled vegetables, tamari, ginger, lemon rind and sunflower seeds. Serve with alfalfa sprouts fluffed along one side.

CREAMY CUCUMBER MILLE FEUILLE

Cool, crisp, smooth and crunchy, this light summer meal will appeal on any occasion. Use wholemeal filo pastry if you can get it.

3 sheets filo pastry
a little oil or melted butter
1 cup cucumber, peeled, diced and drained
1/2 cup each green and red capsicum, diced
2 firm tomatoes, diced and drained
juice of a lemon
1 stick of celery, finely chopped
2 teaspoons chopped chives or parsley
1 cup natural yoghurt
1 cup ricotta cheese or tofu
black pepper
1/4 teaspoon vegetable salt if desired
1 clove crushed garlic
1 avocado
A few raspberries or cherry tomatoes
sprigs of watercress, parsley or sprouts

Brush the filo with the oil or butter and place one sheet on top of the other. Cut into 10 cm x 6 cm rectangles. Bake at 180°C for 5 minutes. Cool.

Combine the cucumbers, peppers, tomatoes, lemon, celery, chives and yoghurt. Blend the ricotta or tofu until creamy and stir into the cucumber mix with the pepper, vegetable salt and garlic depending on the flavours you prefer. Chill 1/2 an hour.

To serve, place a rectangle of filo on each plate, top with a heaped tablespoon of the vegetable mixture, repeat the layers and top with the remaining pastry.

Slice the avocado and decorate each plate with 3 avocado slices, a few raspberries or cherry tomatoes and a sprig of watercress, parsley or sprouts.

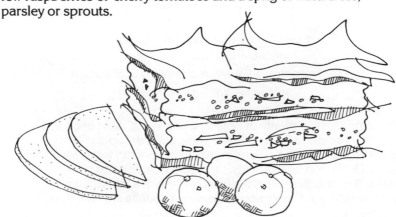

CRUNCHY NUTTY COLESLAW

A traditional salad with a few unusual additions.

1 cup sultanas
1/2 cup freshly squeezed orange juice
2 cups finely shredded cabbage
1 cup bean shoots
1 cup celery, sliced on the diagonal
1 cup carrot, cut in very thin matchsticks
1 tablespoon chopped parsley
1/2 cup zucchini, cut in very thin matchsticks
1/2 cup toasted hazelnuts, chopped
1 cup natural yoghurt (goat's, soy or cow's milk yoghurt can be used)
1/4 cup crunchy peanut butter
1 teaspoon tahini
fresh orange slices for garnish

Soak the sultanas in the orange juice for 30 minutes. Drain and combine with the vegetables, parsley and hazelnuts. Stir together the yoghurt, peanut butter, and tahini until smooth. This dressing can be stirred through the salad, or served alongside it. Garnish with fresh orange slices.

CUCUMBER MOUSSE

1 long continental cucumber
2 cups ricotta cheese
1/2 cup yoghurt
1 1/2 tablespoons agar-agar powder
1/2 cup water
juice of a lemon
a little vegetable salt
freshly ground black pepper
extra thinly sliced cucumber to garnish

Beat together the ricotta cheese and yoghurt in a food processor or blender until creamy. Sprinkle the agar-agar over the water and heat until the powder is completely dissolved. Grate the unpeeled cucumber and drain off any liquid. Mix the cucumber with the ricotta, lemon juice, vegetable salt, pepper and dissolved agar-agar. Stir well and pour into a lightly oiled mould. Chill until set then unmould gently onto a serving plate. Decorate with the extra cucumber slices.

EGGPLANT AND SPINACH MOUSSE

For a light lunch or an appealing centre dish on a table, serve with wholemeal or fingers of rye toast.

2 medium eggplants, peeled and chopped
1/2 bunch spinach, well washed and chopped
1 tablespoon agar-agar powder
1/2 cup hot water
squeeze of lemon juice
a little grated nutmeg
1 clove crushed garlic
2 cups ricotta cheese or mashed tofu
1/2 cup yoghurt
black pepper
1/4 teaspoon vegetable salt if liked, or 1/2 teaspoon tamari
4 large mushrooms, cut into strips
a few spinach leaves
a few watercress leaves or some alfalfa sprouts

Steam the eggplants for 5 minutes, then add the spinach and steam another 5 minutes. Drain and cool.
Dissolve the agar-agar in the hot water and lemon juice. Simmer for 1 minute.

In a food processor blend the eggplant mixture, agar-agar, nutmeg, garlic, ricotta, yoghurt, pepper and vegetable salt or tamari. Pour into 4 individual moulds. Chill until set.
Unmould onto serving and decorate with the mushrooms, spinach leaves, watercress or sprouts around the plate.

GREEK VEGETABLE SALAD

2 cups baby onions, peeled
2 cups green beans (about 20)
2 cups button mushrooms
2 green and 2 yellow zucchini, thinly sliced on the diagonal
1 cup snow peas, trimmed
1 eggplant, thinly sliced
6 radishes, cut in halves
1 punnet cherry tomatoes
DRESSING
2 cloves garlic, crushed
1 tablespoon cider vinegar
1/2-1 tablespoon oil
1/2 teaspoon tamari
black pepper
pinch of tumeric
1 tablespoon toasted pinenuts
a little shredded orange peel

Blanch the baby onions in boiling water for 2-3 minutes. Drain.
Steam the beans, mushrooms, zucchini, snow peas and eggplant
for 2-3 minutes or until barely tender.
Cool immediately. Combine all of the vegetable ingredients
together.
For the dressing mix together the garlic, vinegar, oil, tamari, pepper
and tumeric. Toss this through the vegetables and serve with the
pinenuts and orange peel scattered over the top.

GREEN SALAD PLATE WITH RICOTTA BALLS

½ cup sesame seeds
2 cups ricotta cheese
½ tablespoon chopped fresh herbs, or ½ teaspoon dried
pinch of dry mustard
1 teaspoon tomato chutney (optional)
1 green lettuce
1 cup snow peas
1 large green capsicum, cut in strips
2 sticks of celery, sliced each 3 cm on the diagonal
2 medium zucchini, thinly sliced lengthwise
6 whole baby spring onions
1 teaspoon oil
1 teaspoon lemon juice

Dry toast the sesame seeds in the oven. Mix together the ricotta cheese, herbs, mustard, chutney and sesame seeds. Roll into small balls (3cm). Arrange the lettuce, snow peas, pepper strips, celery slices, zucchini slices, and spring onions on a serving dish. Sprinkle the oil and lemon juice over. Place the ricotta balls to one side to serve.

MIXED UP VEGETABLE SALAD

Always a delight with any meal.

½ lettuce, broken into bite sized pieces

1 cup coarsely grated carrot

1 cup diced cucumber

1 capsicum, cut in strips

1 cup sliced celery

½ cup sliced radishes

1 avocado, peeled and diced

6 spring onions, chopped

4 firm tomatoes, chopped

½ cup sliced mushrooms

1 cup tiny cauliflower pieces

2 teaspoons oil

juice of ½ a lemon

2 teaspoons cider vinegar

pinch of mustard

¼ teaspoon tamari or vegetable salt

1 tablespoon chopped parsley

Prepare all of the salad vegetables and pile into a large bowl. Mix together the oil, lemon juice, cider vinegar, mustard and tamari. Add this to the salad along with the parsley. Toss well and pile carefully into a salad bowl to serve.

MUSHROOM AND GREEN SALAD

One of my favourites and oh-so-healthy!

1 bunch of spinach, very well washed
2 cups of mushrooms, thinly sliced
2 zucchini, thinly sliced
2 sticks of celery, sliced finely on the diagonal
1/2 lettuce, washed and broken into bite size pieces
1 cup of alfalfa sprouts
1 tablespoon chopped parsley
1/2 cup toasted sunflower seeds
1 tablespoon oil
juice of a lemon
2 teaspoons cider vinegar
1 clove of crushed garlic
2 teaspoons tamari
black pepper

Tear the spinach into bite size pieces. Toss together the spinach, mushrooms, zucchini, celery, lettuce, alfalfa sprouts, parsley and sunflower seeds. Combine the remaining ingredients and mix well. Pour this over the salad, toss and serve.
A lovely salad at any time of the year.

MUSHROOM, POTATO AND SNOW PEA SALAD

500 g red skinned or new potatoes unpeeled

1 cup snow peas, topped and tailed

2 cups button mushrooms, cut in halves

1 green capsicum, cut into strips

1 stalk celery, sliced on a diagonal

lettuce leaves, mignonette or red lettuce are best

1 tablespoon chopped parsley

DRESSING

1 tablespoon oil

1 tablespoon cider vinegar

juice of a lemon

1/2 teaspoon dried oregano

1/2 teaspoon tamari

black pepper

Scrub the potatoes and steam for 10-12 minutes.
Blanch the snow peas in boiling water for about 30 seconds, drain and cool.
Put the potatoes, cut in half, the snow peas, mushrooms, capsicum and celery into a bowl. Combine the ingredients for the dressing and put it over the vegetables. Toss well. Arrange the lettuce leaves on a salad plate and pile the vegetables along the centre. Sprinkle with parsley and serve.

PEANUT STUFFED TOMATOES

These always look appealing when served on a salad platter. The same filling ingredients can be used for celery sticks.

1 tomato per person
½ cup of peanut butter
1 cup of mashed tofu or ricotta cheese
¼ cup finely chopped dates
1 tablespoon chopped raisins
3 tablespoons toasted sunflower seeds
1 teaspoon tomato chutney
1 tablespoon finely chopped celery

Slice the base off each tomato and scoop out the insides. Turn upside down to drain. Combine the remaining ingredients, and pile into the tomato shells, place the lids back on to serve.

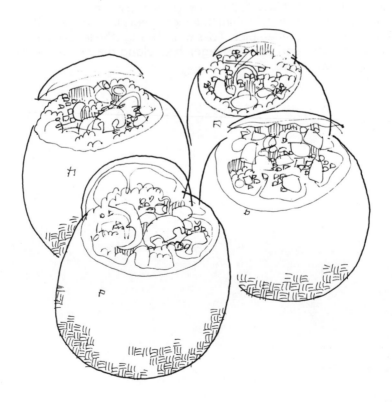

RED CABBAGE, WALNUT AND FETTA SALAD

¼ red cabbage
¼ green spring cabbage
1 tablespoon oil
½ tablespoon lemon juice
½ teaspoon tamari
black pepper
1 cup walnuts
1 cup fetta cheese cubes

Trim the cabbages and shred very finely. Combine the oil, lemon, tamari and pepper. Toss the dressing into the salad and set aside for an hour. Just prior to serving, toss the fetta and walnuts through the cabbages.

SALAD SUPREME

Exotic and unbeatable.

½ tablespoon oil
½ tablespoon cider vinegar
juice of ½ a lemon
¼ teaspoon vegetable salt
pinch of dry mustard
pinch of paprika
2 just ripe avocadoes
2 just ripe mangoes
2 cups snow peas
chives

Mix together the oil, vinegar, lemon juice, salt, mustard and paprika. Peel and thinly slice the avocadoes and mangoes. Arrange the avocado and mango slices on a serving plate with the snow peas. Sprinkle the dressing over the salad. Tie the chives in loose knots and scatter a few over the salad. Serve.

SPICY BANANA IN YOGHURT
– for Curries

Cool and smooth. Just perfect for a hot curry.

1 teaspoon cumin seeds
1 cup natural yoghurt
juice of a lemon, strained
1/2 teaspoon vegetable salt
3 ripe bananas, sliced

Heat the cumin seeds in a dry frypan over a low heat, until golden. Cool. Combine the yoghurt, lemon juice, salt and sliced bananas. Crush the cumin seeds and sprinkle them over the yoghurt mixture before serving.

SPINACH AND HAZELNUT SALAD SUPREME

Unusual, appealing, a delight to look at and a refreshing change for a winter salad.

3 tablespoons chopped hazelnuts
12 green beans, shredded with a bean slicer
1/2 cup watercress sprigs, snipped cress or alfalfa sprouts
8 leaves mignonette or red lettuce (radicchio)
3 cups small or broken spinach leaves
1 crisp green pear, thinly sliced
juice of 1/2 a lemon
1 cup natural yoghurt
black pepper

Dry roast the hazelnuts in a moderate oven until they smell irresistible and are golden in colour. When cooled, rub between your hands to rub off the loose skins.
Blanch the green beans in boling water for 30 seconds, drain and rinse in cold water.
Arrange the watercress or sprouts and lettuce leaves on a plate. Over the top place the green beans and spinach leaves. Brush the pear slices with lemon juice and arrange on the plate. Spoon the yoghurt over the centre, top with ground black pepper and the toasted hazelnuts. Serve.

SPRING SALAD

3 small beetroots, unpeeled
1 butter or romano lettuce, washed
1 mignonette lettuce, washed
½ bunch spring onions
½ bunch radishes
½ bunch watercress
1 cup alfalfa sprouts
DRESSING
1 tablespoon cider vinegar
juice of a lemon
½-1 tablespoon oil
½ teaspoon mustard
½ teaspoon tamari
black pepper

Place the beetroots on a dry baking tray and bake in a moderate oven for 50-60 minutes. Cool, peel and cut them into quarters. Tear the lettuce leaves into bite sized pieces if they are large. Arrange all salad ingredients in a bowl.

Whisk together the dressing ingredients and pour the mixture over the salad just prior to serving. Toss well.

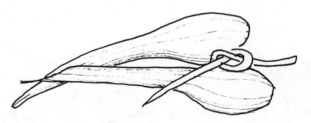

VEGETABLE PASTA SALAD

Pasta has a lot of food value if it is made with mixed whole grains. Used wisely, it can balance a meal.

1½ cups wholemeal pasta shapes
juice of a lemon
½ tablespoon cold pressed oil
½ teaspoon tamari
1 tablespoon chopped fresh basil or ½ teaspoon dried
1 tablespoon each chopped parsley and watercress
black pepper
2 carrots, cut in very thin matchsticks
2 zucchini, cut in very thin rings
4 radishes, thinly sliced
1 red capsicum, diced
6 spring onions, chopped
½ cup toasted pine nuts

Cook the pasta in plenty of boiling water, a little oil in the water will prevent the pasta sticking together. Drain the pasta and while still warm, toss with the lemon juice, oil and tamari. Cool. Add the remaining ingredients except the pine nuts, and toss thoroughly. Serve chilled with the toasted pine nuts scattered on top.

Hot vegetable dishes and main courses

AVOCADO ADVENTURE BURGERS

Certainly a surprise package of little goodies.

1 large, ripe avocado
1 cup ricotta or cottage cheese or well mashed tofu
$\frac{1}{2}$ tablespoon oil
1 leek, very finely chopped
$\frac{1}{2}$ teaspoon each tumeric, cumin and coriander
1 cup finely chopped spinach
$\frac{3}{4}$ cup each grated carrot, zucchini and pumpkin
1 tablespoon chopped parsley
1 tablespoon each toasted sesame and sunflower seeds
$\frac{1}{2}$ cup cornmeal or soy flour
2 teaspoons tamari

Mash the avocado and ricotta together very well. Heat the oil in a frypan and lightly fry the leeks, tumeric, cumin and coriander for 3 to 4 minutes. To this add the spinach, stir well, then the carrot, zucchini and pumpkin. Stir over a high heat for 4 to 5 minutes. Take off the heat and mix in all of the remaining ingredients including the avocado mixture. If it seems a little too moist, add extra cornmeal or soy flour. Form into patties. These can either be baked on a lightly oiled tray or fried in a hot oiled frypan.

Decorate with thin avocado slices brushed with lemon juice. Super delicious served with steamed vegetables or salad, and baked potatoes.

BAKED PUMPKIN TREASURE WITH MUSHROOMS AND ALMONDS

Always a spectacular dish to serve. It adds colour to a vegetarian meal. If you do not have all the spices handy, one teaspoon of curry powder can be used instead.

1 good sized butternut pumpkin
2 teaspoons oil
¼ teaspoon each tumeric, coriander, ground ginger and cumin
1 cup small cauliflower pieces
1 cup small broccoli pieces
10-12 french beans cut in 3 cm lengths
3 zucchini in 1 cm thick slices
16-20 snow peas
16-20 button mushrooms thinly sliced
1 teaspoon tamari
black pepper
¾ cup whole blanched almonds – roasted on a dry baking tray in the oven

Cut the pumpkin in half lengthwise and scoop out the seeds. Scoop out small balls of pumpkin flesh with a melon ball cutter or small spoon, leaving 2 cm of flesh intact around the edge of the shell. Place the pumpkin shells in an ovenproof pan with a small quantity of water and bake in a moderate oven for 30 minutes or until the pumpkin shells are tender.

In a large saucepan heat the oil and carefully fry the spices, add the cauliflower pieces and pumpkin balls together with a little water and cook for 3-4 minutes. Add the broccoli pieces, beans and zucchini, stir well and cook a further 3 minutes. Add the snow peas and mushrooms, heat through and stir through the tamari and pepper. Add the roasted almonds leaving a few aside.

Pile the vegetables into the pumpkin shells, scatter a few almonds over the top, reheat and serve with hot brown rice and a green salad.

A small whole blue skinned pumpkin can be used instead. Cut the top off the pumpkin with a large sharp knife to make lid, scrape out the seeds and continue as above.

BEAN CURRY

A hearty warming winter night meal.

1 tablespoon oil
½ teaspoon of each of the following spices: cumin, ginger, tumeric, mustard, coriander, cinnamon, paprika, cardamon *or 2 teaspoons curry powder*
2 cloves crushed garlic
2 onions, diced
2 leeks, sliced
1 cup each chopped pumpkin and cauliflower
1 cup water
½ cup each sliced celery and beans
½ cup each grated carrot and zucchini
2 cups cooked chick peas or soybeans
1 tablespoon sultanas
½ tablespoon cornflour
½ cup water
2 teaspoons tamari
1 cup chopped broccoli flowers
½ cup green peas

Heat the oil in a large saucepan, add the spices, garlic, onions and leeks and stir while cooking over a moderate heat for 3 to 4 minutes. Add the pumpkin, cauliflower and water, then simmer for 5 minutes. Add the remaining vegetables, chick peas or soybeans and sultanas. Simmer a further 5 minutes. Combine the cornflour and tamari with the ½ cup cup of water. Stir into the curried vegetables along with the broccoli flowers and green peas. Simmer 5 minutes and serve.

Excellent with pappadams, brown rice and tomato chutney.

BEAN GREEN VEGETABLE STEW

Served with baked potatoes or brown rice this makes a complete meal. If you haven't soaked the soybeans ahead of time, put them in a saucepan with plenty of cold water, bring them to the boil, cover and stand for 2 hours. Do not add any salt to the beans as this toughens the outer skin.

½ cup dried soybeans, soaked overnight
2 onions, finely chopped
2 cloves garlic, crushed
½ cup water
1 teaspoon cumin
½ teaspoon each coriander and oregano
1 red capsicum, diced
2 sticks celery, sliced
1½ cups water
1 cup green peas
250 g green beans, cut in 4-5 cm pieces
2 cups broccoli pieces, flowers and stems
2 zucchini thinly sliced
2 teaspoons tamari
black pepper
1 tablespoon chopped parsley

Drain the soybeans, and bring them to the boil in a large pan of water, skimming off any froth that rises to the top. Simmer for 1 hour. Drain.

Cook the onions and garlic in the half cup of water, add the cumin, coriander, oregano and capsicum and cook 5 minutes. Add the celery, water, peas, beans, broccoli and zucchini. Cover and simmer for 8-10 minutes. Stir in the tamari, pepper and parsley. Serve.

This stew can be thickened with a little wholemeal flour or cornflour blended with ¼ cup water and stirred into the simmering stew. Stir well.

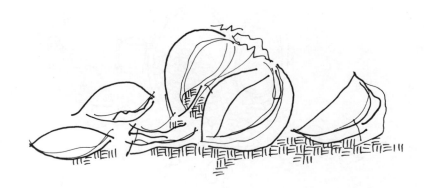

BROCCOLI BEWITCHED

A simple and lovely vegetable casserole.

4 cups broccoli flowers
4 cups cooked brown rice
2 cups mushrooms, thinly sliced
1 avocado, peeled and thinly sliced
1 tablespoon oil
2 tablespoons unbleached white flour
1 1/2 cups milk or soy milk
1/2 teaspoon vegetable salt
1/2 cup oats
1/2 cup sesame seeds
1 tablespoon sunflower seeds
1/2 cup fresh wholemeal breadcrumbs
1 tablespoon wholemeal flour
1 tablespoon tahini

Steam the broccoli until just tender. Place half of the brown rice in a casserole dish. Then layer half of the broccoli, half of the mushrooms, and half of the avocado slices on top. In a saucepan combine the oil and flour, heat for 1 minute, stir in the milk off the heat, then bring to the boil, simmer one minute and stir in the vegetable salt. Pour half of the sauce over the vegetables. Repeat using the remaining foods and sauce. To make the crumble, combine the oats, sesame and sunflower seeds, breadcrumbs, flour and tahini. Spread over the casserole and bake in a moderate oven for 20 minutes.

BROCCOLI IN GINGER ALMOND SAUCE

A tangy and different way to serve broccoli.

½ cup almonds
2 teaspoons oil
½ teaspoon grated fresh ginger
grated rind of ½ a lemon
3 cups broccoli flowers
½ teaspoon tamari, soy sauce
2 tablespoons water

Chop the almonds. Heat the oil, ginger and almonds in a fry pan, cook for 2-3 minutes. Add the lemon rind and broccoli, and cook gently for 1 minute. Add the tamari and water, take care as it will sizzle. Cover and cook for 5 minutes until the broccoli is just crisp. Serve at once with brown rice and a main course dish.

CAULIFLOWER CURRY

The combination of spices used here gives a whole, rich, satisfying flavour, while the coconut milk gives the sauce a delightful creamy consistency. Tempeh, a flat cake of cooked soybeans, is available in some health food shops, or can be substituted by the other ingredients listed.

2 teaspoons oil
2 leeks, finely sliced
1 clove of crushed garlic
1 teaspoon of freshly grated ginger (or 1/2 teaspoon dried)
5 whole cloves
1/4 teaspoon each cinnamon and cayenne
1/2 teaspoon mustard
1 teaspoon each cumin, tumeric and coriander
1 cup of water
1 cup of coconut milk, or 1/2 cup of pieces of creamed block coconut
1/2 cup cashews
4 cups of cauliflower pieces
2 cups of broccoli pieces
1 cup of green peas
2 teaspoons tamari or 1 of vegetable salt
1 cup of 2 cm cubes of tempeh, tofu, or 3/4 cup of almonds

Heat the oil and lightly fry the leeks, garlic and ginger for 2 minutes. Add the remaining spices and stir over a moderate heat for 2 to 3 minutes. Add the water, coconut milk, cashews and vegetables and simmer covered for about 8 minutes. Add a little extra water during this time if necessary. Add the tamari and tempeh, cover and simmer a further 2 to 3 minutes. If the sauce is not thick enough, 2 rounded teaspoons of arrowroot dissolved in a tablespoon of cold water can be added. Heat well and serve sprinkled with a few parsley sprigs.

This is a delightful warming dish. When served with brown rice and a salad you have a well balanced meal.

CHINESE STYLE VEGETABLES

In this quickly cooked dish all the vegetables need to be prepared before you start heating the oil. The vegetables used here serve only as a guide. Be adventurous!

1 tablespoon vegetable oil
1 green and one red capsicum, cut into strips
4 stalks celery, sliced on the diagonal
2 carrots, cut in thin matchsticks
³/₄ cup small cauliflower pieces
¹/₂ cup small broccoli pieces
6 spring onions, cut into 2 cm lengths
2 cm piece fresh root ginger, chopped finely
¹/₂ to 1 teaspoon Chinese five-spice powder
1 cup thinly sliced mushrooms
2 tablespoons chopped parsley
1 teaspoon tamari

Heat the oil in a wok, add all the vegetables, except the mushrooms and parsley and cook,, stirring all the time until the vegetables are tender but still crisp (3 to 5 minutes). Add the five-spice powder, mushrooms, parsley and tamari. Cook for a further 2 minutes. Serve with brown rice or wholemeal noodles, and steamed green beans or peas.

CORN AND MUSHROOM TART

An unusual and nutritious pastry complements this tasty tart.

COTTAGE CHEESE PASTRY

2 cups wholemeal plain flour

2 teaspoons oil

²/₃ cup cottage cheese

¹/₂-³/₄ cup warm water

Sift the flour into a bowl, make a well in the centre, add the oil and cottage cheese to the mix adding enough warm water to make firm dough. Lift on to a lightly floured bench and knead a little. This dough may be difficult to roll out so press it into the tart tin.

FILLING

2 teaspoons oil

6 spring onions, chopped

1 clove garlic, crushed

¹/₂ teaspoon tumeric

2 cups chopped mushrooms

1 cup cooked corn kernels

³/₄ cup grated zucchini

1¹/₂ cups cottage or ricotta cheese

1 tablespoon tahini

2 teaspoons tamari or ¹/₂ of vegetable salt

1 tablespoon chopped parsley

¹/₂ cup wholemeal flour

Heat the oil and cook the spring onions, garlic, tumeric and mushrooms for 5 minutes. Put this into a bowl and add all of the remaining ingredients mixing very well. Pile into the lined tart tin and bake in a moderate oven for 25 to 30 minutes. Decorate with thinly sliced tomatoes. Heat for 3 to 4 minutes and serve.

Excellent for lunch, or as a main meal with a salad. Good with steamed broccoli and a tahini dressing.

CURRIED PEAS AND CAULIFLOWER
WITH TOFU

This is wonderful when served piping hot on a chilly night with warm parathas. If you do not wish to use the combination of spices, 1 or 2 teaspoons curry powder can be used instead.

1 kg fresh peas in the pod
1 tablespoon oil
1 large onion, finely chopped
2 cloves chopped garlic
2 teaspoons fresh grated ginger, or 1 teaspoon dried ginger
1 teaspoon each coriander, cumin and tumeric
½ teaspoon each cardamon and cinnamon
¼ teaspoon each nutmeg and ground cloves
black pepper
3 ripe tomatoes, chopped
3 cups small cauliflower pieces
1 teaspoon tamari
1 cup diced tofu pieces

Shell the peas. Heat the oil in a large saucepan and cook the onion and garlic for 2-3 minutes over a low heat. Add the ginger and remaining spices and stir for 1 minute. Add the tomatoes and simmer 5 minutes. Add the cauliflower pieces and peas, cover and simmer for 6-8 minutes until the vegetables are just tender. Stir in the tamari and tofu and serve.

Diced potatoes can be used instead of the cauliflower.

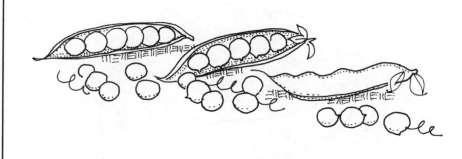

DREAMY CREAMY VEGETABLES

This absolutely dreamy vegetable sauce was created to satisfy my desire for thick creamy sauces while maintaining a completely healthy diet. It can be used with various other vegetarian dishes such as pasta, patties, nut loaves, etc. Here it is combined with lightly cooked diced vegetables. For a richer flavour some curry powder, spices or herbs can be added to the sauce when it is being blended.

³⁄₄ cup carrot, finely diced
1 cup pumpkin, finely diced
³⁄₄ cup celery, sliced
³⁄₄ cup green peas
¹⁄₂ cup sliced green beans
³⁄₄ cup each small cauliflower and broccoli pieces
1¹⁄₂ cups tofu pieces
1 full tablespoon cornflour
2 teaspoons tamari
2 cups cold water
¹⁄₂ tablespoon chopped parsley

Prepare all of the vegetables and steam until just tender, 6-8 minutes. In a blender or food processor, put the tofu, cornflour and tamari. Start to process and gradually pour in the water until the mixture reaches a thick creamy consistency. Pour it into a saucepan and heat while stirring until it comes to the boil. Add a little extra water if it becomes too thick. Simmer for 1 minute. Combine the sauce with the vegetables and parsley.

Serve hot with toast triangles for a lovely light lunch, or with rice or pasta and salad for dinner.

DYNAMIC DUO

The flavoursome vegetables team well with the mashed potato topping. A favourite at Leon and Jan's this recipe is printed with thanks.

1 tablespoon water
2 onions finely chopped
2 cloves garlic
2 zucchini, cut in 1 cm thick chunks
1 large eggplant, in large dice
2 cups button mushrooms
4 tomatoes, diced
1 vegetable stock cube or 2 teaspoons tamari
4 potatoes, peeled
1 tablespoon sesame seeds
1/2 cup fresh breadcrumbs

Heat the water in a large pan and cook the onions and garlic for 5 minutes. Add the zucchini, eggplant, mushrooms and tomatoes along with a little water and the stock cube or tamari and cook, stirring occasionally for 6-8 minutes. Dice the potatoes and steam or simmer until tender. Pile the vegetables into a casserole dish. Puree the potato and spread over the vegetables. Sprinkle with sesame seeds and breadcrumbs and bake in a moderate oven for 10 minutes.

Serve with a green salad.

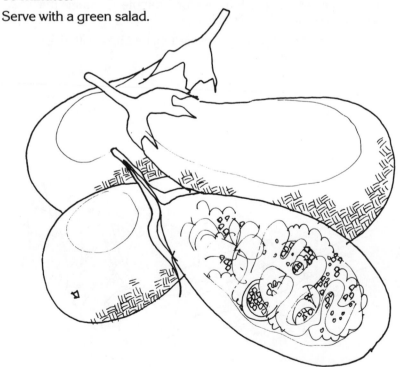

EGGPLANT AND MUSHROOM LASAGNE

This makes a tasty and satisfying meal served with a green salad and steamed broccoli.

½ tablespoon oil
1 teaspoon tamari
juice of ½ a lemon
2 large eggplants
250 g mushrooms, thinly sliced
1 packet instant wholemeal lasagne noodles
TOMATO SAUCE
2 teaspoons oil
2 large onions, finely chopped
2 cloves garlic, crushed
½ teaspoon tumeric
1 kg ripe tomatoes, chopped
1 teaspoon each oregano and basil
1 tablespoon tomato flakes
1 tablespoon chopped parsley
1 teaspoon tamari
black pepper
WHITE SAUCE
1 tablespoon oil
1 tablespoon each wholemeal plain and unbleached white flour
1 ½ cups milk or soy milk
1 teaspoon tamari
black pepper

Combine the oil, tamari and lemon juice. Cut the eggplant into 1 cm thick slices and lay them on a foil fined tray. Brush the slices with the oil mixture and grill both sides until golden brown.

To make the sauce, heat the oil in a saucepan and cook the onions, garlic, and tumeric for 5 minutes. Add the tomatoes, oregano, basil and tomato flakes. Stir well then simmer for 15-20 minutes. Add the parsley, tamari and pepper.

Lightly oil a casserole dish and cover the base with a third of the tomato sauce. Cover this with a layer of the lasagne noodles and then cover with half of the grilled eggplant slices and mushrooms. Repeat these layers making sure the lasagne noodles are well covered and moist with the sauce. Finish with the remaining tomato sauce.

To make the white sauce, blend the oil and flours together in a saucepan and stir over a low heat for 3-4 minutes. Add the milk and stir until it boils for 2 minutes. Stir in the tamari and pepper. Pour this sauce over the lasagne and bake in a moderate oven for 30 minutes.

EGGPLANT AND MUSHROOM SAUCE WITH NOODLES

This sauce goes well with whole grain shell or ribbon noodles.

½-1 tablespoon oil
1 clove garlic, crushed
2 eggplants, diced
2 cups mushrooms, chopped
4 zucchini, sliced
2 tablespoons chopped parsley
1 teaspoon dried oregano
1 teaspoon tamari
pasta

Heat the oil in a saucepan and lightly cook the garlic and eggplants for 3 to 5 minutes, stirring well. Add the remaining ingredients and stir occasionally for 6-8 minutes or until the vegetables are just cooked.

Cook the pasta in plenty of boiling water for 10-15 minutes. Drain well. Pile the pasta in a serving dish and spoon the sauce over to serve. Alfalfa sprouts on the side add colour.

GADO GADO

A popular Indonesian and Malaysian salad, Gado-Gado is traditionally a mixture of raw and cooked vegetables attractively arranged in layers on a large platter and served with a spicy peanut sauce. The vegetables suggested here are a guide, make use of whatever is in season.

SAUCE
2 cups unsalted roasted peanuts
1 tablespoon peanut or vegetable oil
1 onion, finely chopped
2 cloves crushed garlic
1 green or red capsicum, finely chopped
1 teaspoon tumeric
½ teaspoon each cumin, coriander and mustard **or** 1 teaspoon of curry powder can be used instead of the spices
2 teaspoons honey
juice of a lemon
1 teaspoon tamari
1 cup coconut milk
1 cup water

Put the peanuts in a blender or food processor and grind coarsely. Heat the oil in a frypan, add the onion, garlic, capsicum and spices and stir while cooking for 2-3 minutes. Add the ground peanuts, honey, lemon juice and tamari. Stir well. Stir in the coconut milk and water, reduce the heat and simmer the sauce until it is smooth, but not too thick to be poured. Set aside.

VEGETABLES

2 large potatoes, boiled and diced
2 cabbage leaves, shredded and very lightly steamed
3 carrots, thinly sliced lengthwise and very lightly steamed '
2 cups green beans, cut into 3 cm pieces and very lightly steamed
3 small zucchini, lightly steamed
2 cups spinach, steamed and chopped lengthwise
2 cups bean sprouts
1 cup alfalfa sprouts
1 small cucumber, thinly sliced
1 cup celery, sliced on the diagonal
1 tablespoon oil
1 cup tofu cubes marinated in a little tamari
2 onions, finely sliced in half rings

Arrange the vegetables on a platter in layers beginning with the potatoes, cabbage, carrots, beans, zucchini, spinach, sprouts, cucumber and celery. Heat the oil in a frypan and lightly fry the tofu cubes. Set them aside and fry the onions. Scatter the tofu over the vegetables, and the fried onions over the top of this.

Served with the peanut sauce alongside and brown rice this is a meal in itself.

GOLDEN BUTTERNUT PUMPKIN PIE

For something different and appealing an unusual rice crust adds texture and variety to this tasty pie. Ideal for people on a wheat free diet, but make sure the cornflour used is pure maize cornflour. If you do not have all the spices listed 1 to 2 teaspoons of curry powder can be substituted.

RICE CRUST

3 cups cooked brown rice (short grain rice binds well)
½ cup sesame seeds
1 large tablespoon tahini
⅓ cup cornflour
½-1 tablespoon oil
2 teaspoons tamari

Combine all of these ingredients and mix together well. If it does not hold together add a little extra tahini and cornflour. Pat into the base and sides of a well oiled pie dish. Bake in a moderate oven for 10-15 minutes until lightly golden.

FILLING

2 butternut pumpkins
2 cups of ricotta or tofu (optional)
2 teaspoons oil
2 onions, finely chopped
½ teaspoon each tumeric, ginger, mustard, coriander and cumin
1 cup zucchini, finely diced
1 cup celery, finely chopped
⅔ cup green peas
1 cup hot water
1 tablespoon kuzi or arrowroot
2 tablespoons cold water
2 teaspoons tamari or as desired

Cut the pumpkins in half lengthwise and bake cut side down on an oiled tray in a hot oven for 30 minutes, or until very soft when tested with a skewer. Cool a little and scoop out the inside (discarding the seeds) and puree the pulp in a blender. At this stage 2 cups of tofu or ricotta cheese can be blended with the pumpkin for a firmer texture. Heat the oil in a large saucepan and lightly fry the onion for 2 to 3 minutes. Add the spices and stir over a moderate heat for 1 to 2 minutes taking care it does not burn. Add the zucchini, celery, and peas along with 1 cup of hot water. It will splatter a little so be careful! Stir to lift the spices off the base of the pan and simmer the mixture until the water has evaporated.

Dissolve the kuzu or arrowroot in the cold water, stir this into the vegetable mixture, add the tamari, and simmer one minute. Pour the vegetable mixture over the rice base. Spread the pumpkin puree over the top of this.

Bake in a moderately hot oven for 20 to 25 minutes. Decorate with thinly sliced apple dusted with a little cinnamon or nutmeg and heat a further 5 minutes. Allow the pie to stand for 5 minutes before serving.

A very tasty and filling pie this would go well served with a crisp green salad with nuts or sunflower seeds and cubes of tofu marinated in tamari. Some lightly steamed broccoli or cauliflower would be good too. A protein rich dessert would completely balance this meal.

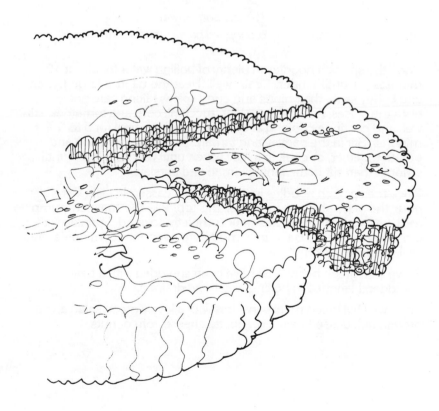

GREAT FRIENDS

*This recipe grew out of one lovely night with some wonderful friends.
The combination of flavours is just great.*

1 packet (up to 500 g) flat ribbon spinach noodles
2 teaspoons oil
2 onions, diced
2 teaspoons of curry powder, or a mixture of curry spices such as cumin, coriander, tumeric, mustard, ginger and paprika
3 cups eggplant, finely chopped
2 cups zucchini, finely chopped
1 cup sweetcorn kernels
4 tomatoes, chopped
1 tablespoon chopped parsley
2 teaspoons tamari
TOPPING
1 1/2 cups each chopped pumpkin and potato
1 tablespoon tahini
1/2 teaspoon tamari
1/2 tablespoon each chopped parsley and sesame seeds

Cook the spinach noodles in plenty of boiling water for about 10 minutes, or until tender. Drain well. Heat the oil in a large frypan and lightly saute the onions and curry spices taking care not to burn the spices. Add the eggplant, zucchini, corn and tomatoes, stir well and continue cooking at a moderately high heat for 5 to 6 minutes. Stir in the parsley and tamari. Steam the pumpkin and potato together, or cook in a little water, until very soft. Mash until smooth then stir in the tahini, tamari and parsley.

Place the spinach noodles in the base of a casserole dish. Carefully pour the vegetable mixture over the top. Pile the mashed pumpkin mixture over the vegetables until completly covered. Sprinkle with the sesame seeds. Bake in a moderate oven for 15 minutes until well heated through.

Serve with green beans that have been shredded with a bean shredder, blanched in boiling water and drained.

For a well balanced meal serve this with a lovely green salad and a protein rich dessert based on ricotta cheese, tofu or nuts.

HOT SPICED BEETROOT

3 beetroots

pinch of ground cayenne

pinch of ground paprika

2 tablespoons cider vinegar

2 teaspoons honey

1 teaspoon cracked black pepper

Place the unpeeled beetroots on a dry baking tray and bake in a moderate oven for one hour or until tender when tested with a skewer. Cool a little, peel with a knife, and dice. Combine the diced beetroot with the remaining ingredients in a saucepan. Toss over a gentle heat for 3-5 minutes or until well heated. Serve as a accompaniment to a main course dish.

MEXICAN STYLE CHOKOS

4 chokos

1 teaspoon oil or water

1 clove garlic, sliced

2 onions, chopped

1 leek, thinly sliced (optional)

4 large tomatoes, chopped

1/4 teaspoon paprika

pinch of ground chilli or a little diced chilli

2 teaspoons chopped parsley

6 green or black olives

black pepper

Peel and slice the chokos and steam for 10 minutes. Heat the oil or water and cook the garlic, onions and leeks for 5 minutes. Add the tomatoes and choko slices. Cover and cook gently for 5-10 minutes. Sprinkle with the paprika, chilli, parsley, olives and pepper and serve.

LEEK AND SPINACH TART WITH RICE CRUST

The delectable rice crust makes this leek tart so good to eat.

CRUST
1½ cups long grain brown rice
½ cup sesame seeds
1-2 tablespoons tahini
½ cup wholemeal flour or cornflour
2-3 teaspoons tamari

FILLING
1 tablespoon oil or water
3 leeks, washed, halved, and finely sliced
2 cloves garlic, crushed
1 bunch spinach, well washed and shredded
1 tablespoon oil, extra
full ½ cup unbleached white flour
1½ cups liquid (milk or water)
2 teaspoons tamari
black pepper

To make the crust, cook the rice in boiling water until quite soft (this will take from 40-50 minutes), drain well but do not rinse through. Mix all of the crust ingredients together and press into the base and sides of a lightly oiled 24 cm flan tin. Chill while making filling.

To make the filling, heat the oil or water and cook the leeks and garlic slowly for about 15 minutes. Add the spinach and cook a further 5 minutes. Take another saucepan, blend the oil and flour in it. Heat until bubbly then stir in the liquid, tamari and pepper. Bring to the boil and cook for one minute while stirring to make a thick white sauce. Combine the leeks and sauce. Pile the mixture into the rice crust and bake in a moderate oven for 15-20 minutes. Some grated cheese can be sprinkled on top if desired for a golden finish.

'NASI GORENG'

An interesting adaptation of one of the best known Indonesian rice dishes.

4 thin slices of tofu
1 teaspoon tamari
1 tablespoon oil
3 onions, finely chopped
2 cloves garlic, crushed
1 bunch spring onions, finely sliced
2 red capsicums, diced
¼ teaspoon cayenne or paprika
½ cup each sliced celery, green peas and grated carrot
1 tablespoon chopped parsley
3 cups cooked long grain brown rice
2 teaspoons tamari
black pepper
juice of half a lemon
1 tablespoon peanuts
1 tablespoon sultanas or currants

Lie the tofu slices on a plate and sprinkle with tamari. Set aside. Heat the oil in a large saucepan or frypan and keeping the heat fairly high add the onions, garlic, spring onions and capsicums. Cook while stirring for about 5 minutes or until the onions are clear. Add the cayenne, celery, peas and carrot and cook for another 5 minutes stirring occasionally. Add the parsley, rice, tamari, pepper, lemon juice, peanuts and sultanas. Keep the heat fairly high and stir the mixture for about 5 minutes until it is well heated through. Add just a little more oil if necessary.

Heat another frypan, brush lightly with oil, and fry the tofu slices for 1-2 minutes on each side. Remove and cut into thin strips.

Serve the rice in warm bowls with the tofu slices scattered on top.

Nasi Goreng stands well as a meal on its own, or it can be served with a green salad, or lightly steamed green vegetables.

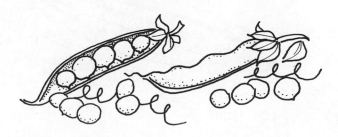

OH WHAT A SPLENDID PIE

This is just superb. A wonderfully interesting potato and pumpkin crust with a tasty vegetable and creamy sauce filling.

THE CRUST

2½ cups potato, chopped
1 cup pumpkin, chopped
½ teaspoon oil
½ teaspoon tamari
½ cup cornmeal or cornflour

Steam the pumpkin and potato, or cook in a little water until quite soft. Drain and mash until smooth, beat with a wooden spoon and add the oil, tamari and cornflour. Mix well. Add a little extra cornflour if the mixture is too moist. Pat into the base and sides of a lightly oiled 22-24 cm pie shell.

FILLING

¾ cup corn kernels
¾ cup green peas
1 cup carrot, diced
1 cup zucchini, diced
1 cup caulfilower pieces
½ cup broccoli pieces **or** any combination of available vegetables

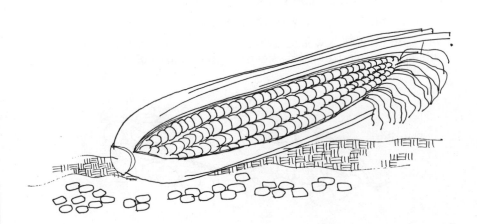

Steam all of the vegetables together for 6 to 8 minutes or until just cooked but still crisp. Remove from the steamer immediately to prevent further cooking.

THE SAUCE

1 tablespoon oil
2 onions, finely diced
1 clove garlic, crushed
½ cup wholemeal plain flour (buckwheat or rice flour can be used here)
3 cups cold water
2 teaspoons tamari
1 tablespoon chopped parsley
2 teaspoons tahini (optional)

Heat the oil in a saucepan and saute the onions and garlic until clear. Stir in the flour and cook for another minute. Add the water, stirring well, and bring to the boil. Stir in the tamari, parsley and tahini.

Combine the vegetables and sauce together. Pile this into the potato crust base. This pie can be baked as it is, or decorated with tomato slices, thin zucchini slices, thin capsicum rings or dried wholemeal breadcrumbs. Bake in a moderate oven for 15 to 20 minutes or until the base is crisp and the vegetables well heated.

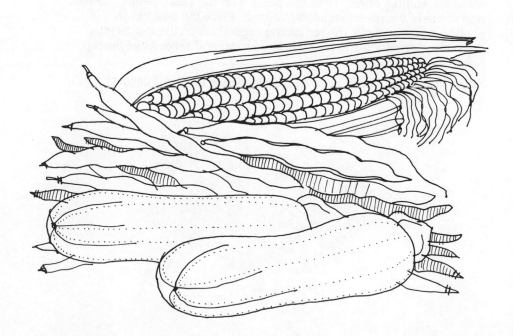

PASTA SUPREME

The secret to prevent pasta clumping together is to add a little oil to the cooking water, or toss it with a little oil as soon as it is drained.

2 zucchini, thinly sliced on the diagonal
2 cups broccoli, cut into flowers
1 cup each snow peas and green peas
2 stalks celery, thinly sliced on the diagonal
6 stalks asparagus, sliced on the diagonal
500 g wholemeal spaghetti or flat noodles
1/2-1 tablespoon oil
2 cloves garlic, crushed
1/2 cup pinenuts
2 cups sliced mushrooms
1/2 punnet cherry tomatoes, cut in halves
1 teaspoon dried, or 1 tablespoon fresh chopped basil
black pepper
a little tamari

Blanch the zucchini, broccoli, snow peas, green peas, celery, and asparagus in boiling water for 2 minutes, drain and rinse under cold water. Cook spaghetti in plenty of boiling water for 10 minutes. Drain. Meanwhile heat oil in a large pan and gently fry garlic and pinenuts for 2-3 minutes. Add mushrooms and tomatoes and fry a further 2-3 minutes. Reserving a little of the tomato mixture for decoration, add the remaining vegetables to the pan and cook for 5 minutes, stirring often. Toss the pasta with the basil, pepper, tamari and some of the green vegetable mixture. Place the pasta in six shallow bowls and pile the remaining vegetables on the top. Scatter the cherry tomatoes and mushrooms on top and serve while piping hot.

Some parmesan cheese can be sprinkled over the top if desired.

POTATO CROQUETTES WITH TOFU FILLING

These croquettes cook better if they can be refrigerated for a couple of hours so allow extra time if you can.

3-4 medium potatoes
2 teaspoons oil or water
1 onion, finely diced
black pepper
8 cubes of tofu, cut in 2 cm dice
2 teaspoons tamari
FOR COATING
breadcrumbs made from stale wholemeal bread, or a little wholemeal flour
a little oil for frying

Steam the potatoes until tender, leave to cool. Peel, sieve or mash very well. Heat the oil or water and cook the onion for 3-4 minutes until soft. Add the onion and pepper to the potato and mix well. Leave to cool. Lie the tofu in a dish and sprinkle with the tamari. Set aside. Divide the potato mix into eight portions. Form into a ball, then flatten out. Drain the tofu and place one piece in the centre of each potato portion. Fold the potato mixture over to cover the tofu, and pat into an even croquette shape. Dip each croquette into breadcrumbs or flour. Refrigerate for a couple of hours if possible. These can be fried in a little oil in a hot frypan turning when they are golden on one side, or cooked in a hot oven (200°C) on a well oiled baking tray for 15 minutes.

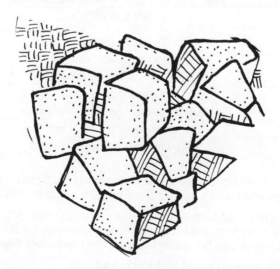

RAINBOWS AND RED CABBAGE

This is something that tastes wonderful, is easy to prepare and looks delightful.

1 tablespoon oil
2 carrots, cut in thin matchsticks
2 leeks thinly sliced in half rings
2 cups pumpkin cut in small thin pieces
1/2 red cabbage thinly sliced
2 sticks celery, thinly sliced
1 tablespoon raisins
1/2 teaspoon each caraway seeds and cinnamon
juice of both a lemon and an orange
1 tablespoon cider vinegar
1 bunch watercress, finely chopped or 3/4 cup sliced spinach
2 teaspoons tamari

Heat the oil in a large pan, add the carrots, leeks and pumpkin and stir while cooking for 5 to 7 minutes. Add the red cabbage, celery, raisins, caraway seeds, cinnamon, lemon and orange juice, and cider vinegar. Mix well, cover and cook on a low heat for 8 to 10 minutes, stirring occasionally. Add the watercress and tamari, cover and heat a further 3 minutes. Serve as a lovely colourful accompaniment to a main meal such as nut patties or a vegetable and nut loaf.

RED KIDNEY BEAN CHILLI

If you like your food hot, this will appeal. With thanks to Jan for this spicy recipe.

1/2-1 tablespoon oil
2 cloves garlic, crushed
2 small onions, finely chopped
4 tomatoes, diced
1 tablespoon or more of chilli sauce
2 cups cooked brown rice
500 g cooked red kidney beans

Heat the oil and cook the garlic and onions for 5 minutes, add the tomatoes and cook a further 3 minutes, stir in the chilli sauce.

Layer the rice and kidney beans in a casserole dish. Pour the chilli sauce over the top and bake in a moderate oven for 20 minutes. Grated cheese can be sprinkled over the top before baking.

Serve with a green salad and hot bread rolls.

SAVOURY PUMPKIN PANCAKE

These tasty pancakes make an enjoyable light meal.

BATTER

2 cups finely grated pumpkin
2 spring onions, finely chopped
1 cup wholemeal plain flour
1 teaspoon tamari or vegetable salt
½-1 cup water
natural yoghurt

Combine the pumpkin and spring onions. Sprinkle with the flour and tamari, and stir in sufficient water to make a thick batter. Heat a little oil in a frypan and fry spoonfuls of the batter, turning when golden. Serve at once with some natural yoghurt on the side.

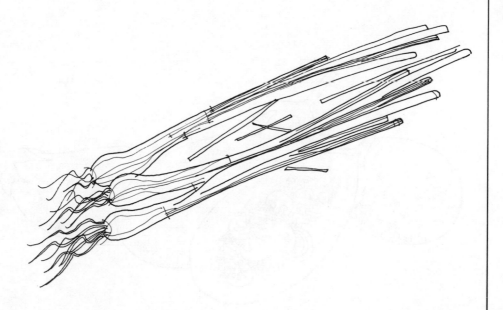

SAVOURY STUFFED EGGPLANT

Stuffed eggplant always looks delightful when served with a green salad, or lightly steamed vegetables.

3 medium sized eggplants
2 tomatoes, chopped
1 onion, very finely chopped
1 clove garlic, crushed
1 green capsicum, chopped
2 cups cooked brown rice
1 tablespoon pine nuts
1 tablespoon currants
1 teaspoon lemon juice
1 teaspoon chopped mint
1 teaspoon tamari
black pepper

Put the eggplants in a large saucepan of cold water and slowly bring to the boil. Simmer for 1 minute only, then remove the eggplant and dunk them in cold water. Cut them in half lengthwise and carefully scoop out the flesh leaving a 1 cm thick shell. Chop the flesh and put it in a saucepan with the tomatoes, onion, garlic and capsicum. Heat while stirring and cook for 5 minutes. Mix this with the remaining ingredients stirring very well. Pile into the eggplant shells and place on a lightly oiled baking tray. Bake in a moderate oven for 15-20 minutes. This can be served either hot or cold.

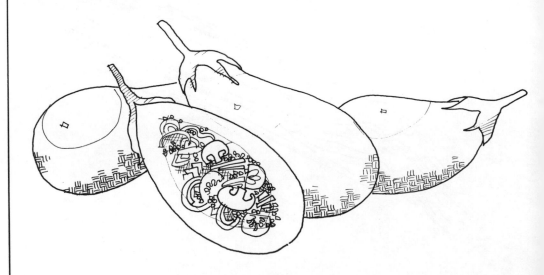

SICILIAN SPAGHETTI

3 large eggplants, cut into 3 mm slices
1 large onion, diced
2 cloves chopped garlic
6 tomatoes, chopped
1/2 teaspoon oregano
2 tablespoons dried tomato flakes
2 small zucchini, diced
1 cup fresh peas
1/2 cup corn
1 cup small broccoli pieces
1 teaspoon tamari
black pepper
250 g wholemeal spaghetti
4 tablespoons dried wholemeal breadcrumbs

Steam the eggplant slices, in small batches or the lower slices will over cook, until just tender. Drain. Cook onion and garlic in a little water for 5 minutes, add tomatoes, oregano, tomato flakes, zucchini, peas, corn and broccoli, stir well, cover and simmer for 5 minutes. Add tamari and pepper. Meanwhile cook spaghetti in boiling water for 10-12 minutes. Drain and combine with the vegetables. Well oil a deep 22 cm cake tin and sprinkle some of the breadcrumbs on the base and side. Place a large slice of eggplant in the centre of the tin. Arrange slices overlapping around base and side of tin. Use spoonfuls of the filling to support the slices as you go. Spoon the remaining filling into the centre and pack it down well. Arrange remaining slices of eggplant, overlapping each slice, to cover the top of the filling completely. Sprinkle with remaining breadcrumbs. Bake uncovered in a moderate oven for 25-30 minutes or until golden brown. Stand a few minutes before turning onto a serving plate. Serve sprinkled with parsley or alfalfa sprouts.

SPAGHETTI 'BOLOGNAISE'

The favourite dish with a difference. What a fine filling meal this makes!

500 g wholemeal spaghetti
1 tablespoon oil
1 clove crushed garlic
2 onions, finely diced
1 green capsicum, chopped
2 cups mushrooms, chopped
5-6 tomatoes, chopped
2 cups cooked brown lentils
1 teaspoon tamari
2 tablespoons chopped parsley
$\frac{1}{2}$ teaspoon dried oregano, or 2 teaspoons fresh oregano
$\frac{1}{4}$ teaspoon dried basil, or 2 teaspoons fresh basil
1 cup tofu or tempeh squares
1 extra teaspoon tamari or $\frac{1}{2}$ teaspoon vegetable salt
2 teaspoons oil
$\frac{1}{2}$ cup chopped almonds

Cook the spaghetti in plenty of boiling water until tender (10-15 minutes). Heat the oil in a frypan and add the garlic and onions, cook while stirring for 3-4 minutes. Add the capsicum and mushrooms and cook a further 3-4 minutes. Then add the tomatoes, brown lentils, tamari, parsley and herbs. Cook for 5 minutes until well heated. Sprinkle the tofu or tempeh squares with a little tamari. Heat the extra oil in a separate frypan and lightly fry the squares until a little coloured on each side. Drain the spaghetti and pile onto the serving plates. Pour the lentil sauce over this, scatter the tofu or tempeh on top, then sprinkle with the almonds. Serve with a salad, or some lightly steamed green vegetables.

SPICY BAKED PUMPKINS

If you can get some small pumpkins this recipe turns dinner into a special event.

4 small pumpkins for baking, or 1 per person

2 teaspoons oil

1 teaspoon curry powder or a mixture of spices

6 spring onions, finely chopped

1 clove garlic, crushed

2 stalks celery, finely chopped

3 firm tomatoes, finely chopped

2½ cups cooked brown rice

1 tablespoon each sunflower seeds, sultanas

1 tablespoon chopped parsley

2 teaspoons tamari

2 teaspoons tomato chutney (optional)

1 cup finely shredded spinach

Cut the tops off the pumpkins and set aside, scoop out the seeds from the insides. Heat the oil in a frypan and lightly cook the curry powder, spring onions, garlic and celery for 3-4 minutes. Add the remaining ingredients and stir through to combine. Pile this mixture into the pumpkin shells and place on a dry baking tray. Bake the pumpkin lids separately. Cook in a moderate oven for 50-60 minutes or until the pumpkin shells feel tender when tested. Place the lids on top. Serve with a tossed salad, or steamed green vegetables.

SPICY SPINACH AND POTATO SIDE DISH

A popular Indian dish this is a simple, yet tasty way of cooking spinach.

1 bunch of spinach or 1 bunch of silverbeet
2 teaspoons oil or water
2 onions, finely sliced
1 green capsicum, finely chopped
1 teaspoon tumeric
1 teaspoon ground ginger
2-3 potatoes peeled and diced

Thoroughly wash and chop the spinach or silverbeet. Steam for 5 minutes or until just cooked. Heat the oil or water in a saucepan, add the onions, capsicum, tumeric and ginger. Stir while cooking for 3 to 4 minutes. Add the potatoes, cover the pan, reduce the heat, and cook, stirring occasionally until the potatoes are just tender. Add the spinach, stir well and cook for a further 3 to 4 minutes, or until the vegetables are fairly dry and well heated.

Serve hot as an accompaniment to a main course dish such as vegetable patties or loaf; or as a filling for small baked pumpkins.

SPINACH PASTA WITH MUSHROOM SAUCE

Ribbon pasta served with this tasty mushroom sauce makes a pleasant and quick meal.

½ tablespoon oil
2 onions, finely chopped
2 cloves of garlic, crushed
1 cup mushrooms, thinly sliced
2 cups chopped tomatoes
½ teaspoon each dried basil and rosemary
black pepper
juice of half a lemon
1 teaspoon tamari
1 packet (up to 500 g) spinach ribbon noddles
chopped parsley

Heat the oil in a saucepan and lightly fry the onion and garlic for about 3 minutes. Add the mushrooms and cook a further 2 to 3 minutes. Add the tomatoes, basil, rosemary, pepper, lemon juice and tamari. Cover and simmer for 15 minutes. Meanwhile cook the noodles in plenty of boiling water for 10-15 minutes. A little oil added to the water will prevent the noodles sticking. Drain thoroughly.

Serve on individual plates with the mushroom sauce over the top. Sprinkle with parsley. Serve with lightly steamed zucchini slices. A few tofu cubes can be added to the sauce just before serving or grated cheese can be sprinkled on top. This will balance the nutritional value of the meal.

SPINACH WALNUT ROLLS IN CITRUS LEMON SAUCE

Tangy and tasty this dish is a pleasure. Rice cooked a day earlier will hold together better.

¾ cup short grain brown rice
4 spring onions, finely chopped
½ cup celery, finely chopped
¾ cup walnuts, finely chopped
1 tablespoon raisins, chopped
½ teaspoon tamari
12 spinach leaves
1 cup fresh strained orange juice
2 tablespoons lemon juice
a little vegetable salt and black pepper if desired
2 teaspoons arrowroot or kuzu blended in a little cold water
a few drops of vinegar to heighten the flavour
1 cup carrot cut in very fine strips
1 cup of leeks, the greener end cut in very fine strips
a few whole walnuts
½ cup celery sliced on the diagonal

Cook the rice in 2 cups of water until it is absorbed and tender. Cool but do not rinse the rice. Combine the rice with the spring onions, celery, walnuts, raisins and tamari. Mix it with your hand and squash it together as you go. If it does not hold together a little tahini can be added to bind it, although it does tend to have a strong flavour. Place a heaped tablespoon of this mixture on the underside of each spinach leaf and roll up. Place the rolls in a frypan with about 5 mm of water in the bottom. Cover and cook for 5 minutes. Combine the orange and lemon juice with the vegetable salt and pepper. Heat, add the blended arrowroot and vinegar and the carrots and leeks, then heat until clear and simmer 2 minutes. Place a little of the vegetable garnish on each serving plate, top with the spinach rolls, remaining vegetable and sauce. Garnish with a few walnuts and celery slices.

SPRING ROLLS

These make use of frozen spring roll pastry. They are a favourite with my sister Sandy's children.

4 cups or ½ bunch silverbeet or spinach well washed and chopped
1 cup grated carrot
1 cup grated zucchini
1 cup ricotta cheese or mashed tofu
½ cup grated low fat or soy cheese if liked
a little grated nutmeg
1 teaspoon tamari, vegetable salt or vegetable flavouring
1 packet frozen Chinese spring roll pastry
DIPPING SAUCE
½ cup tamari or soy sauce
2 tablespoons lemon juice
1 clove garlic, crushed
pinch of ground caraway or dill
pinch of ginger or a little chopped fresh ginger
1 cup bean sprouts

Steam the silverbeet or spinach for 5 minutes, drain and squeeze all of the liquid out. This liquid is too high in vitamins or minerals to waste so add it to a pot of soup or a sauce. Combine the silverbeet with the grated carrot, zucchini, ricotta or tofu, cheese, nutmeg and tamari. Mix well. Separate the spring roll pastry and place a heaped tablespoon of the mixture on the corner of each. Roll up corner to corner tucking in the ends. Place a cake cooling rack on an oven tray and lie the spring rolls on this. Each spring roll can be brushed with a little oil if you like. Bake in a moderate oven for 20 minutes turning the rolls over after 10 minutes to avoid soggy bottoms. Combine all of the ingredients for the dipping sauce and serve in a side bowl. A good tomato sauce to dip them in is popular with children.

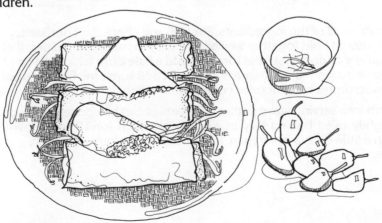

SPRING STEW SIDE DISH

*A simple, colourful and pleasant dish to serve with vegetable patties,
a nut loaf or vegetable pie.*

10-12 baby whole onions, peeled
2 cloves crushed garlic
1/2 cup water
250 g snow peas trimmed if necessary
3 zucchini, thinly sliced on the diagonal
1/2 small lettuce, shredded
1/4 teaspoon dill seed
1 teaspoon tamari

Cook the onions and garlic in a little water for 10 minutes. Add the
snow peas and zucchini, cover and steam for 2-3 minutes, shaking
or stirring if necessary. Add the shredded lettuce, dill and tamari, stir
and cover. Heat through for a further 2 minutes, then serve while
hot and still bright green.

SUPER SCRUMPTIOUS BURGER ROLLS

*Quick and simple, and very, very tasty. These go well when cooked
on a barbecue.*

2 cups tofu, mashed, or ricotta cheese
1/4 cup pumpkin, mashed
1/2 cup each grated carrot and zucchini
1 tablespoon each chopped parsley, sesame seeds and peanut butter
2 teaspoons tahini
1/2 cup buckwheat, soy flour, or wholemeal flour

Combine all of the ingredients. Mix well and check the consistency
as it should hold together well and be easy to make into patties. If it
is too dry or does not hold together add a little extra tahini and/or
peanut butter. If the mixture is too moist add some fresh wholemeal
breadcrumbs, extra flour or cooked brown rice.

Form into serving sized patties. The patties can be cooked either on
a lightly oiled baking tray in a moderate oven for 10 to 12 minutes
or in a little oil in a hot frypan, for about 3 to 4 minutes on each
side.

SUPERNOODLE PANCAKES

Sunday night's dinner at our house is something to look forward to as my daughter has her own choice of food. Here is one Sunday night creation.

PANCAKE BATTER

½ cup buckwheat flour

½ cup wholemeal flour

1 teaspoon cornflour

1 teaspoon oil

soy or cow's milk as needed

1 cup or wholemeal noodles, a mixture of soy and wheat noodles would be good here

Combine the flours in a bowl, add the oil, then add sufficient milk, stirring from the centre out until a smooth, coating batter consistency is reached. The batter should coat the back of a wooden spoon and be the consistency of a thick banana smoothie. Let stand for at least 10 minutes, beat again, and add a little extra milk if necessary. Heat a well oiled frypan and pour in sufficient batter to make pancakes about 10 cm in diameter. When the top is dry and a little firm, turn the pancake over.

Meanwhile prepare the noodles. Put the noodles into boiling water and simmer for about 10 minutes or until they are soft. Drain well.

To serve, place a pancake on each plate, cover with the noodles, place another pancake on top. Serve with tomato sauce and a salad for a fun meal. Be warned, the noodles fall out easily but we're working on it!

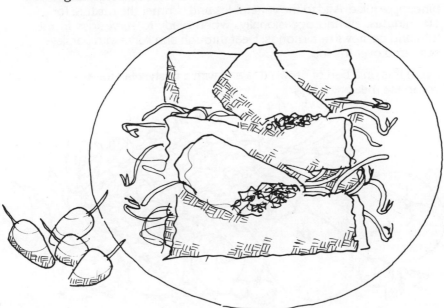

SWEET AND SOUR

Always a favourite, this is a great recipe for a special occasion.

1 tablespoon oil or water can be used
2 onions, cut in strips
1 bunch of spring onions, cut in 2 cm lengths
1 red and 1 green capsicum, cut in strips
12-15 green beans, trimmed and cut in half
1 cup each celery and carrot, cut in matchsticks
3 tomatoes, diced
2 cups ripe pineapple cut in small chunks
1 tablespoon arrowroot
1 cup water
1 tablespoon cider vinegar
2 teaspoons tamari
1 tablespoon honey
1 teaspoon grated fresh ginger, or ½ teaspoon of dried ginger
½ cup pineapple juice
1 cup of tofu cubes, 1 cup of cashews or almonds
chopped parsley

Heat the oil or water and lightly cook the onion, spring onions, red and green capsicum, stirring over a moderate heat for 2 minutes. Add the green beans, celery, carrot, tomatoes, and pineapple. Stir while heating for 1-2 minutes. Blend the arrowroot with the cold water, combine with the cider vinegar, tamari, honey, ginger and pineapple juice. Add to the vegetables and simmer the mixture for 10 minutes, stirring occasionally. When ready to serve toss in the tofu and cashews or almonds. Heat through and serve with parsley scattered over the top.

Serve this on a bed of brown rice and with a fresh salad for a complete meal.

TAGLIATELLE WITH BROCCOLI SAUCE AND WALNUTS

A well flavoured pasta dish is always welcome.

3 cups broccoli pieces
1 cup water
1 cup milk (can be soy milk)
$^{1}/_{2}$ teaspoon vegetable salt or tamari
black pepper
350 g wholemeal tagliatelle
2 teaspoons oil
100g walnuts, coarsely chopped
1 cup tofu cubes
a little extra tamari
1 tablespoon chopped parsley

Chop the broccoli and cook in the water for 6-8 minutes or until soft. Puree it in a food processor adding the milk, vegetable salt or tamari and pepper. Meanwhile cook the tagliatelle in plenty of boiling water, with a little oil, for 10 minutes. Drain. Heat the oil and lightly fry the walnuts and tofu cubes for 2 minutes. Sprinkle with a little extra tamari. Reheat the broccoli sauce. Arrange the pasta on plates and top each serving with the broccoli sauce. Pile some of the walnuts and tofu over this and sprinkle with parsley. Serve with a bowl of parmesan cheese.

TOFU AND POTATO CAKES

Munchy little patties to add texture to a meal.

2 cups tofu
1 cup grated potato
$^{1}/_{2}$ cup grated carrot
2 tablespoons wholemeal flour
1 tablespoon cornflour
2 teaspoons tamari or a little vegetable salt
$^{1}/_{2}$ teaspoon ground peppercorns
a little oil if needed
extra flour for coating

Mash the tofu with a potato masher until like a paste. Mix in the remaining ingredients adding a little oil if it is too dry. Take spoonfuls of the mixture and shape into patties, coating with extra flour.

The patties can be baked on a lightly oiled baking tray in a moderate oven, or fried in a little hot oil in a frypan until golden.

TOFU MOUSSAKA

A delicious eggplant dish with a delightful tofu (or ricotta) cream sauce. This is well worth the effort. Perfect for those who love eggplant.

3 medium eggplants
oil for frying
1 large onion, diced
1 green capsicum, diced
1½ cups sliced mushrooms
2 cloves crushed garlic
8-10 tomatoes, chopped
2 teaspoons tamari or ½ teaspoon vegetable salt
2 teaspoons dried tomato flakes
1 bay leaf
1 teaspoon each oregano and basil
equivalent to 1 cup of tofu slices
Cream Sauce (see below)
¼ teaspoon grated nutmeg

Slice the eggplants into 1 cm thick slices. Cut these in half if they are too large. The eggplant slices can then be lightly fried in a little oil, but work quickly to prevent the eggplant soaking up too much oil. Lie the slices on paper towelling to drain. If not using the oil, steam the eggplant slices for 5 minutes and then cool. Cook the onion and green capsicum in a little water in a saucepan until clear. Add the mushrooms and garlic and cook a further 3 to 4 minutes. Add the tomatoes, tamari, tomato flakes, bayleaf, oregano and basil. Simmer for 10 to 15 minutes. Take a large baking, or casserole dish and place in layers half of each of the eggplant slices, and tomato sauce, and all of the tofu slices. Top this with the remaining eggplant slices and tomato sauce. Spread the Cream Sauce over this and sprinkle the nutmeg on top. Bake uncovered in a moderate oven for 35 minutes.

CREAM SAUCE

2 cups of tofu, or ricotta cheese
1 tablespoon of lemon juice
2 teaspoons of oil
1 tablespoon of wholemeal flour
2 tablespoons of parsley, chopped
2 teaspoons of tamari or a little vegetable salt

Simply blend all of these ingredients together until smooth.

Tofu Moussaka goes well served with baked potatoes or brown rice, and a green salad.

TOFU RICE BURGERS

Simple to make and tasty, these burgers are always a good standby.
Brown rice cooked the day before always holds together better.

1½ cups cooked brown rice

1½ cups mashed tofu

½ cup wholemeal, or soy flour

2 tablespoons chopped parsley

½ cup each finely chopped spring onions and celery

½ cup each grated carrot and zucchini

1 clove crushed garlic

½ teaspoon cumin

1 teaspoon dried basil or thyme, or 1 tablespoon if
using the fresh herbs

2 teaspoons tamari or ½ teaspoon vegetable salt

1 tablespoon tahini

sesame seeds for coating

Combine all of these ingredients, except the sesame seeds. Form into patties, add extra tahini if it does not hold together well, and coat with the sesame seeds. Place on an oiled baking tray and bake in a moderate oven for 20 to 25 minutes.

Serve with fine strips of raw carrot alongside, a green salad or a steamed green vegetable.

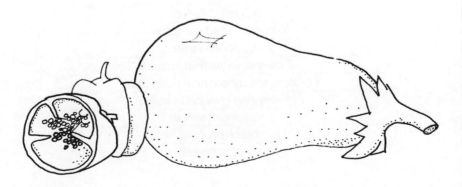

VEGETABLE PIE WITH SPICE AND RICE

A very warming, filling, tasty and nutritious pie.

RICE CRUST

3 cups cooked brown rice (short grain rice is best)

1/2 cup sesame seeds

1 large tablespoon tahini

1/2 cup cornflour

1 tablespoon oil

2 teaspoons tamari

FILLING

1/2 tablespoon oil

1 clove garlic, crushed

2 onions, diced

1/2 teaspoon tumeric
or 2 teaspoons of curry powder can be used instead of the spices listed below:

1/2 teaspoon each ginger, coriander, cumin, mustard and cinnamon

1/4 teaspoon each paprika and cardamon

1 cup each pumpkin and zucchini, diced

3/4 cup green peas

3/4 cup carrot, diced

1 cup cauliflower or broccoli pieces

3/4 cup celery, sliced

a little water

1/2 cup coconut milk

1 tablespoon cornflour

2 teaspoons tamari

TOPPING

1 cup mashed tofu

1/2 cup mashed pumpkin

2 teaspoons tahini

2 teaspoons peanut butter

1 tablespoon wholemeal plain flour

1 tablespoon chopped parsley

2 teaspoons tamari

black pepper

1 packet pappadams

TO MAKE THE CRUST

Combine all of the crust ingredients and mix together well. If it does not hold together well add a little extra tahini and cornflour. Pat into the base and sides of a well oiled pie dish. Bake in a moderate oven for 10-15 minutes until lightly golden.

TO MAKE THE FILLING

In a large saucepan, heat the oil, add the onions and garlic and cook 2 to 3 minutes. Add the spices and stir over a moderate heat for another 2 to 3 minutes. Add the prepared vegetables, a little water to cover the bottom, and the coconut milk. Stir to mix the spices evenly. Cover and simmer for about 8 to 10 minutes stirring occasionally and adding a little extra water if necessary. Combine the cornflour and tamari with a little cold water and stir it into the vegetables. Heat and stir until it boils. Pour the vegetables over the rice crust.

TO MAKE THE TOPPING

Put all of the ingredients (apart from the pappadams) in a food processor and blend until smooth. Spread the topping over the vegetable pie. Bake in a moderate oven for 10 to 12 minutes or until well heated and golden on top.

Cut the pappadams into 5 mm wide strips with scissors. Heat a little oil and add the pappadam strips, turning with tongs after a few seconds and cooking until the strips are crisp. Drain on absorbent paper and serve alongside the pie.

VEGETABLE PANCAKES

A real favourite with children. The wheat and buckwheat flour combined with the milk and vegetables gives a good nutritional balance.

½ cup wholemeal self-raising flour
¼ cup buckwheat flour
1 cup or more of milk (soy or cow's milk)
½ cup corn kernels, cooked
½ cup each grated carrot and zucchini
1 cup finely chopped spinach leaves
1 tablespoon chopped parsley
1 teaspoon tamari
a little vegetable oil

Combine the flours in a bowl and blend in the milk until a smooth batter is obtained. Add the vegetables, parsley and tamari, mixing very well. Heat a little oil in a frypan. Drop spoonfuls of the vegetable pancake mixture into the frypan and cook until lightly browned on both sides.

With a good quality tomato sauce, these make a great snack.

VEGIE FILO PARCELS

A delightful entree or light meal.

¹/₄ cup water
1 leek and one onion finely chopped
1 clove crushed garlic
1 cup each finely diced potato and pumpkin
¹/₂ cup sweet corn kernels
2 sticks celery, finely sliced
1 avocado (still a little firm), diced
pinch of cayenne
fresh black pepper
juice of half a lemon
¹/₄ teaspoon vegetable salt, optional
filo pastry
8-10 chives, briefly blanched
extra avocado slices for garnish

Heat the water and cook the leek, onion and garlic for 5 minutes.
Add the potato, pumpkin and corn and cook for a further 5
minutes, stirring occasionally and adding a little more water if
necessary. Add the celery, avocado, cayenne, pepper, lemon juice,
vegetable salt and heat through. Set aside to cool. Oil one sheet of
filo, cut into four quarters and place one on top of the other. Place
two tablespoons of the mixture on top. Gently bring the corners up
to form a parcel. Tie with string and place on a dry baking tray.
Bake at 190°C for 12-15 minutes until golden and crisp. You may
need to reduce the temperature towards the end of cooking time to
prevent the tops burning. Remove the string and tie each with a
single strand of chive. Garnish with extra avocado slices and short
lengths of chives.

Serve with Herb or Tofu Mayonnaise or perhaps with White Sauce.

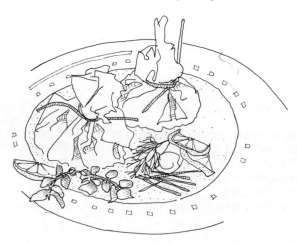

VERY HERBY PIE

Chewy rice on the base, tangy vegetables in the middle, and a creamy smooth sauce on the top. This is great.

1 cup water
2 onions and 2 potatoes, diced
1 cup each carrot, zucchini and pumpkin, diced
1 cup green peas
1 cup sliced celery
1 tablespoon chopped fresh basil, or ½ teaspoon dried basil
1 tablespoon chopped fresh coriander, or ½ teaspoon dried coriander
1 tablespoon chopped parsley
2 teaspoons chopped rosemary, or a pinch of dried rosemary
2 teaspoons tamari
3 cups cooked brown rice
2 cups mashed tofu, or ricotta cheese
2 teaspoons tahini or peanut butter

Cook the onions in a large saucepan in just a little of the water until they are cooked (2 to 3 minutes). Add the remaining vegetables, water and herbs. Cook for 10 minutes stirring occasionally. Stir in the tamari. Spoon the rice into the base of a casserole dish, cover with the vegetable mixture. Blend together the tofu, or ricotta, with the tahini and/or the peanut butter. Spread this over the vegetable mixture and bake in a moderate oven for 10 to 15 minutes until well heated.

Serve with hot wholemeal garlic bread.

WALNUT AND VEGETABLE ROULADE

A dinner party delight. This is always immensely popular, so be prepared for second helpings.

PASTRY

2 cups wholemeal plain flour
2-3 tablespoons margarine
2 teaspoons oil
warm water to mix
extra flour for rolling

Rub the margarine into the flour until it resembles breadcrumbs. Add the oil and water and mix until a soft moist dough is formed. Turn onto a well floured bench and knead lightly until it is a smooth soft dough. Halve the dough and roll each piece out thinly to a size approximately 250 mm square.

FILLING

2 teaspoons oil
2 onions and 2 leeks, finely chopped
¾ cup each grated potato and pumpkin
1 cup green peas
¾ cup sweetcorn kernels
2 cups finely chopped spinach
¾ cup finely chopped walnuts
1 tablespoon sunflower seeds
½ cup tahini
2 teaspoons tamari
(¾ cup grated tofu or ricotta cheese is an optional addition)

Heat the oil in a large pan and lightly saute the onion and leeks until clear. Add the potato, pumpkin, peas, corn and spinach. Cook for 5 minutes stirring occasionally. Remove from the heat and stir in the walnuts, sunflower seeds, tahini and tamari. Cool a little . Spread an even layer of the vegetable mixture completely over each pastry square.

Starting from the closest edge carefully roll up the pastry so that the pastry and vegetable filling looks like a swiss roll. Place on a lightly oiled baking tray, brush the top of the pastry with a little water and sprinkle with sesame seeds. Bake in a moderately hot oven for 20 to 25 minutes.

Serve slices of the roularde with a lovely tossed lettuce and sprout salad, some snow peas and a lemon flavoured tahini dressing.

WALNUT AND VEGETABLE STRUDEL

A light meal that is not only delicious but also perfectly nutritious providing foods from all of the food groups.

³/₄ cup grated pumpkin
1 cup each grated zucchini and carrot
2 sticks celery, finely sliced
1 cup finely shredded broccoli
¹/₂ cup finely shredded cauliflower
¹/₂ cup broken walnuts
¹/₂ cup chopped raisins
2 cups cottage cheese, ricotta or mashed tofu
1 cup cooked soybeans (optional)
2 teaspoons tamari
¹/₄ teaspoon dill
filo pastry, wholemeal if available
extra walnuts for decoration
parsley sprigs or alfalfa sprouts

Put a little water into a large pan and add the grated pumpkin, zucchini and carrot. Stir and cook for 5 minutes. Add the celery, broccoli and cauliflower and cook a further 5 minutes or until lightly cooked adding a little extra water if necessary. Stir in the walnuts, raisins, cottage cheese, soybeans, tamari and dill. Mix well and cool.

Lay out 4 sheets of filo pastry and brush lightly with oil between each sheet. Lay the pastry on a lightly oiled baking tray. Spread the filling along one length of the pastry leaving a 2 cm edge. Fold this up then fold over the large edge of pastry tucking in the ends. Brush the top with a little oil. Bake in a moderate oven 190°C for 20 minutes or until the pastry is golden. You may need to turn the temperature down a little towards the end of the baking time if it is cooking too quickly. Slice into wedges and serve with a home made tomato sauce around the edge and decorate with extra whole walnuts and parsley sprigs or alfalfa sprouts.

WALNUT BALLS WITH TOFU LEMON CREAM SAUCE

Simply delectable. Add some colour by decorating with thin slivers of lemon rind and serving with a spinach salad, grilled herbed tomatoes, and mashed potato or wholegrain noodles.

2 cups finely chopped walnuts
1 onion, finely chopped
½ cup whole grain fresh breadcrumbs
3 tablespoons chopped parsley
1 cup tofu
2 tablespoons water
juice of a lemon
1 clove crushed garlic
½ teaspoon mustard
1 teaspoon tamari
¼ cup wholemeal flour

Lightly cook the onion in a little water. With this combine 1½ cups of the walnuts, the breadcrumbs and parsley. Process the remaining ingredients in a blender until smooth, and combine with the nut mixture. Form into small walnut sized balls, rolling in the reserved nuts. Place in a lightly oiled oven-proof dish, and bake in a moderate oven for 20-25 minutes. Serve hot with Tofu Lemon Cream Sauce.

TOFU LEMON CREAM SAUCE

1 cup tofu
juice of 2 lemons
¾ cup water
1 tablespoon arrowroot or kuzu
2 tablespoons chopped parsley
1 teaspoon tamari

Process the tofu and lemon juice in a blender until smooth. Heat the water in saucepan. Dissolve the arrowroot in a little extra water and add to the saucepan, stirring until thickened. Stir in the blended tofu, parsley, and tamari. Pour over the walnut balls and serve.

Desserts

ALMOND APRICOT SUPREME

This dessert is extremely delicious and so easy to prepare. Just right for special occasions.

2 tablespoons cornflour or kuzu
$^1/_2$ cup cold water
3 cups soy milk (cow's milk, or a mixture can be used)
$^1/_2$-1 tablespoon honey
$^1/_2$ cup finely chopped raisins
$^1/_2$ cup finely chopped dried apricots
$^1/_2$ teaspoon vanilla essence
grated rind of 1 lemon
juice of $^1/_2$ a lemon
1$^1/_2$ cups almond meal
1 teaspoon tahini
toasted shredded almonds

Dissolve the cornflour or kuzu in the cold water. Stir in the soy milk and honey. Bring to the boil while stirring constantly, then simmer for 1-2 minutes while still stirring. Remove from the heat and quickly stir in the raisins, apricots and vanilla essence. Pour into a mixing bowl and add the lemon rind and juice, the almond meal and tahini. Extra almond meal can be added for a stiffer consisentency. Spoon into serving dishes and decorate with toasted slivered almonds.

Almond apricot supreme is best when served on its own.

APPLE AND WALNUT STRUDEL

It's nice to know that delightful desserts can still be good for us.

4 large cooking apples
juice of ½ a lemon
½ teaspoon cinnamon
6 sheets of filo pastry
oil or melted margarine
½-1 tablespoon honey or natural apricot jam sweetened with honey
½ cup each raisins and chopped walnuts

Peel, core and thinly slice the apples, sprinkle with the lemon juice and cinnamon. Lie 2 sheets of filo pastry on top of each other. Brush with the oil, lie two more sheets on top. Brush with oil and place the remaining two sheets on top. Brush this with the honey or apricot jam. Spread the sliced apples along the longest edge of the pastry a little in from the edge. Sprinkle evenly with the raisins and walnuts. Roll the shorter edge up and the remaining pastry over the top of the apples, sealing with a little water. Tuck the ends in. Place on a lightly oiled baking tray and bake in a moderately hot oven for 15 to 20 minutes until golden.

Serve with creamy natural yoghurt and extra walnuts. Place apple wedges dipped in lemon juice on the side.

APPLE CUSTARD PIE

A tasty oatmeal crust combined with a creamy apple filling make this pie a sweet delight.

OATMEAL PASTRY

1 cup rolled oats
1 cup plain flour
¾ cup cottage cheese or mashed tofu
luke warm water to mix

FILLING

3 tablespoons cornflour
a little cold water
2 cups soy or cow's milk
2 teaspoons honey (optional)
½ teaspoon vanilla essence
grated rind of 1 lemon
¼ teaspoon each grated nutmeg and cinnamon
3 cups grated unpeeled green apples

To make the pastry, combine the oats and flour in a bowl, add the cottage cheese or tofu and mix a little with your fingertips. While mixing add enough water to make a soft, but not sticky dough. Knead a little on a lightly floured bench, then press into a 20-22 cm flan or pie tin. Bake in a moderately hot oven for 10 minutes or until dry and golden. Cool.

Combine the cornflour and water in a saucepan. Stir in the milk and honey. While stirring bring to the boil and simmer for one minute. Stir in the vanilla, lemon rind, nutmeg, cinnamon and apples. Pour this into the pie shell and chill. Serve decorated with thin strips of lemon rind.

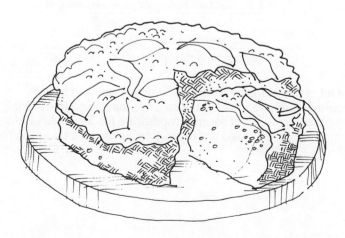

APRICOT AND PAW-PAW PARADISE

A delightful way to start or finish a meal when presented with fresh fruit sections and wholemeal biscuits.

½ cup finely chopped dried apricots
3 tablespoons fresh orange juice
¼ teaspoon ground ginger
1 tablespoon chopped dried paw-paw
2 tablespoons almond meal
½ teaspoon grated orange rind
1½ cups ricotta cheese or pureed tofu
2 teaspoons honey (optional)
½ cup toasted flaked almonds or poppy seeds

Place the apricots, orange juice and ginger in a small saucepan. Simmer over a low heat until the apricots soften. Stir in the paw-paw, almond meal and orange rind. Cool. Stir the apricot mixture with the ricotta or tofu, and honey. Spoon onto the centre of a plate and shape into a large circle and flatten the top. Cover with poppy seeds or the toasted almonds. Chill.

Serve with sliced fresh fruit and whole wheat biscuits. A few daisies on the side look delightful.

BANANA AND HAZELNUT ICECREAM SUPREME

A treat for any time of the year.

6 large ripe bananas
1 tablespoon cold pressed oil
½-1 tablespoon honey or pure maple syrup
¾ cup soy or cow's milk
2 teaspoons vanilla essence
2 tablespoons roasted chopped hazelnuts

Place all of the ingredients in a food processor and blend thoroughly until creamy. Pour into a container and freeze for 2 to 3 hours. Allow to stand at room temperature for 5 minutes before serving. Serve decorated with strawberries or extra chopped roasted hazelnuts. Delightful.

BANANA AND ORANGE PANCAKES

A popular dessert with a sweet, tasty, healthy difference.

2 tablespoons buckwheat flour
¹/₂ tablespoon pure cornflour
2 tablespoons wholemeal flour or brown rice flour
¹/₂ teaspoon oil
1¹/₂-2 cups milk, soy milk can be used
2 tablespoons fresh orange juice
3 oranges, peeled and segmented
3 bananas, peeled and sliced

Combine the buckwheat flour, cornflour and wholemeal flour. Mix in the oil and milk until a creamy coating batter is obained. Heat a little oil in a small frypan. When very hot, thinly coat the base of the pan with the pancake batter. When one side is golden brown turn it over and cook the other side. Turn onto a plate. Repeat making more pancakes and stacking them on top of each other. Heat the orange juice and stir in the fruit pieces. Heat through. Divide this over each pancake, fold and serve immediately. A few toasted slivered almonds can be scattered over the top.

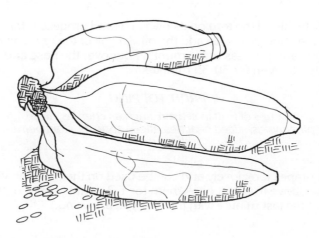

CHEESECAKE DELIGHT

Don't let the name confuse you, as this cheesecake can be made completely without any dairy products for a delightful protein rich, nutritious dessert.

BASE

¾ cup rolled oats, ground in a blender until fine
1 cup coconut
½ cup soy flour, or wholemeal flour
1 tablespoon of honey
1 tablespoon of sesame seeds
½ cup melted margarine (milk free margarine or oil can be used)
hot water to mix

Combine all of these ingredients mixing well, and adding sufficient hot water to make the mixture moist, but holding together well. Pack into a 22 cm spring form pan and bake in a moderate oven for 10 minutes. As soy flour browns at a low temperature take care during this baking as it may darken around the edges too quickly.

FILLING

2 cups of tofu, or 2 cups of ricotta cheese, or creamy cottage cheese
1 tablespoon of oil, if using the tofu
¾ cup soy or cow's milk yoghurt
¼-½ cup honey
1 teaspoon vanilla essence
1 teaspoon each grated lemon and orange rind
1 tablespoon of fresh orange juice
2 tablespoons arrowroot

If using tofu, blend the tofu on its own in a food processor for about ½ a minute, then gradually add the oil. Add all of the remaining ingredients and process until smooth. Pour over the base and bake in a moderate oven for 30-35 minutes.

FRUIT TOPPING

2 cups of fruit in season, such as cherries, diced pineapples, sliced peaches, sliced apricots, strawberries, sliced pears

(Sultana grapes look lovely and can be used on their own or with any of the above fruit, but cook them for 1-2 minutes only, or toss them in at the last minute with the fruit you are using.)

¾ tablespoon of water
½ tablespoon of honey if desired
1 tablespoon of arrowroot dissolved in a little extra cold water
1 teaspoon of lemon juice

Cook the fruit with the water and honey over a low heat for 5 minutes. Add the dissolved arrowroot and lemon juice and stir for 1-2 minutes until it thickens. Carefully spoon on top of the pie for the last 5 minutes of baking time. Chill several hours before serving. This looks lovely with little thin matchstick strips of orange or lemon rind sprinkled on top. Serve with Tofu Cream or Ricotta Cream.

CREAMY APRICOT ICECREAM

A delicious summer icecream. Use fresh apricots when they are in season.

2 teaspoon agar-agar powder
2 cups apricot nectar or apple juice
3 cups mashed tofu
2 tablespoons chopped dried apricots soaked in a little water, or 1 cup chopped fresh, ripe apricots
½-1 tablespoon honey
2 teaspoons pure vanilla essence

Sprinkle the agar-agar powder over the apricot nectar in a small saucepan. Heat and stir until the agar-agar dissolves. Cool a little. Blend the tofu until creamy in a food processor. Add the agar-agar mixture and remaining ingredients. Blend until smooth. Freeze for 2 hours. Remove, blend again and freeze. Chopped, lightly cooked pears can be used in place of the apricots.

CREAMY SMOOTH DESSERT BALLS

These are light, creamy and just delicious, nutritious, little sweet snacks.

1 cup tofu, or ricotta cheese
½ tablespoon of oil
½ teaspoon of lemon juice
1 tablespoon each chopped dates and raisins
grated rind of both a lemon and an orange
¼ teaspoon cinnamon
½ teaspoon vanilla
1 tablespoon chopped almonds
2 cups desiccated coconut

If using the tofu blend it in a food processor with the oil and lemon juice. Combine all of the remaining ingredients together mixing very well. A little honey can be added for a sweeter flavour, or a little tahini for a slightly nutty flavour. Roll the mixture into small balls and refrigerate.
Although these will keep for 5-7 days refrigerated, they are difficult to resist.

DEEP DISH PLUM PIE

A special summer surprise, this is perfect.

PASTRY
125 g each wholemeal self-raising flour and unbleached white flour
150 g butter or margarine
2 teaspoons oil
2 teaspoons honey
warm water to mix

FILLING
1 kg fresh plums
900 ml water
1 tablespoon honey
2 tablespoons tapioca
grated rind of a lemon
1 tablespoon natural apricot jam
½ tablespoon cornflour

Sift flours into a bowl and rub in the butter or margarine. Add the oil and honey and enough warm water to make a firm dough. Knead a little on a lightly floured board, then roll out two thirds of the pastry to line a deep 20 cm pie dish.

Halve and stone the plums. Heat the water and honey and poach the plums for 10 minutes. Drain thoroughly reserving the liquid. Arrange the plums on top of the pastry and sprinkle with the tapioca and lemon rind. Roll out the remaining pastry to a 22 cm circle and cover the pie dish, crimping the edges. Make pastry petals for the centre. Bake in a moderate oven at about 190°C, for 45 minutes. Just prior to serving heat the apricot jam and brush over the top of the pie to make it glisten. Dissolve the cornflour in a little cold water and blend into the plum syrup. Heat and stir until it thickens and boils. Serve warm with the plum pie.

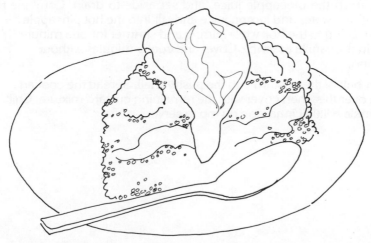

DESERT SUN PINEAPPLE PIE

A most unusual, yet delightfully refreshing pie.

PASTRY

1 cup each wholemeal plain flour and unbleached white flour
½ cup margarine
1 teaspoon oil
1 teaspoon honey
warm water to mix

Combine the wholemeal and white flour in a bowl and rub in the margarine until the mixture resembles breadcrumbs. Add the oil and honey, then mix in the warm water until a soft and slightly sticky dough is formed. Put onto a well floured board, knead lightly until it is smooth and not sticky. Roll out thinly and cut to line a 23-25 cm pie dish. Bake in a moderate oven for 10 minutes, or until cooked. Cool.

FILLING

1½ cups pineapple juice
1 tablespoon honey (optional)
3 cups cooking apples, peeled and cut into thick slices
3 cups fresh pineapple pieces, diced
3 tablespoons cornflour
3 tablespoons water
1 teaspoon lemon juice
½ teaspoon vanilla essence
a little cinnamon

Combine the pineapple juice and honey in a saucepan, bring to the boil and stir to dissolve the honey. Add the apples and pineapple pieces and simmer until just tender (5-6 minutes). Carefully lift the fruit from the pineapple juice, and set aside to drain. Combine the cornflour, water and lemon juice and stir into the hot pineapple juice. Bring to the boil while stirring and simmer for one minute. Stir in the vanilla essence. Cover and cool 5 minutes without stirring.

Pour half of the custard into the pastry shell. Spread the cooked fruit over this, then cover with the remaining custard mixture. Chill. Sprinkle a little cinnamon on top to serve.

DRIED FRUIT DELIGHT

A warm and nourishing dessert for a cold winter's night.

10-12 prunes without stones
10-12 dried apricot halves
1/2 cup chopped dried apple
1/2 cup raisins
3 bananas, peeled and sliced
4 tablespoons fresh orange juice
grated rind and juice of a lemon

Soak the prunes, apricots and dried apple overnight in just enough water to cover. Drain the fruit and place it in an ovenproof dish with the raisins and bananas. Stir in the orange juice, lemon rind and lemon juice. Bake in a moderate oven for 15-20 minutes.

Serve with creamy natural yoghurt.

FROZEN FRUITZ

Very refreshing for a hot summer evening.

2 cups cooked pureed fruit such as apricots, peaches, pears, apples, plums, prunes etc.
2 cups natural yoghurt using soy, goat's, or cow's milk yoghurt
1/2-1 tablespoon honey
1 teaspoon vanilla essence

Blend all of these ingredients together. Freeze in trays until mushy. Beat and freeze again. Serve topped with toasted slivered almonds, or toasted shredded coconut.

FRUIT AND WALNUT WHIP

Using whatever fruits are in season, this makes an interesting breakfast or dessert dish.

½ kg apples, pears, or clingstone peaches, or a combination of these
2 cups ricotta cheese or mashed tofu
½ cup yoghurt
½ cup chopped walnuts
½ cup each sultanas and chopped raisins
1 teaspoon each grated orange and lemon rind
½ teaspoon cinnamon
a little grated nutmeg

Peel the apples or pears and cook in a little water until soft. Cool then combine with the ricotta or tofu and yoghurt (if using the tofu, blend it in a food processor first until creamy). These ingredients can be combined in a food processor for a creamier consistency. Add all the remaining ingredients, except the nutmeg, and mix well. A little honey can be added for a sweeter taste.

Serve with the nutmeg sprinkled on top, on its own, with fresh or lightly cooked fruit, or as a breakfast dish with muesli. A few walnut halves make a pleasant decoration.

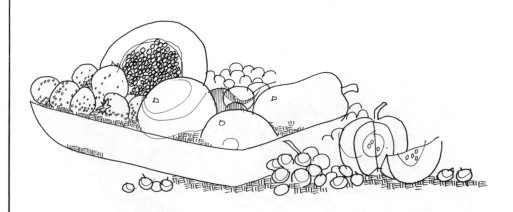

GOLDEN APRICOT STEAMED PUDDING

A steamed pudding that is light, packed with healthy foods, tangy and good for you! Sounds too good to be true. Try this!

1½ cups chopped dried apricots

1 cup sultanas

½ cup finely chopped walnuts

1 carrot, grated (approximately 1 small cup)

grated rind of both an orange and a lemon

¼ cup wholemeal flour

2 cups fresh wholemeal breadcrumbs

60 g margarine, or ¼ cup oil can be used

½ cup natural apricot jam or marmalade sweetened with honey

¼ cup fresh orange juice

Combine together the apricots, sultanas, walnuts, grated carrot, orange and lemon rind, flour and breadcrumbs. Cream the margarine until light and beat in the jam. Add to the dry ingredients along with the orange juice. Mix well. Spoon into an oiled one litre pudding basin. Cover with oiled foil or greaseproof paper. Place basin in a large saucepan with enough water to reach half-way up the basin sides. Boil for 2 hours, checking and adding extra boiling water as required. Serve warm with milk, soy milk, or a honey custard.

GREEN FRUIT SALAD

Cool and refreshing on a warm late summer's night.

1 small honeydew melon

250 g white seedless grapes

4 kiwi fruit

juice of a lemon

2 cups natural yoghurt

½ cup slivered almonds

Cut melon in half and remove the seeds. Dice the flesh or press out balls with a melon baller. Separate and wash the grapes. Peel and halve the kiwi fruit and cut into thin slices. Combine the fruits with the lemon juice and chill. Serve in chilled dessert glasses and hand the yoghurt, sprinkled with slivered almonds, separately.

HONEY WHOLEMEAL PLUM PUDDING

A traditional plum pudding with a very healthy twist. As this contains no eggs and is low in fat it may break a little when sliced for serving. But a good dollop of custard on top, a cheery smile, and the taste buds will win over.

2½ cups wholemeal plain flour
1 teaspoon mixed spice
½ teaspoon cinnamon and nutmeg
¼ teaspoon ground ginger
2 cups fresh wholemeal breadcrumbs
½ cup each chopped almonds and dates
½ cup each sultanas, currants and raisins
½ cup mixed peel
¼ cup milk, preferably soy milk
3 tablespoons oil, good quality margarine or butter whichever you prefer
1 cup honey
2 teaspoons bi-carb soda
1 cup grated carrot
½ cup grated zucchini
1 tablespoon brandy or soy milk
1 teaspoon pure vanilla essence
juice and grated rind of 1 orange

Sift flour and spices and combine with breadcrumbs, almonds, dried fruit and peel. Put the milk on to heat with the honey and butter or oil. Heat until dissolved without boiling. While still hot add the soda, it will froth, but immediately mix it into the dry ingredients along with the carrot, zucchini, brandy or extra milk, vanilla essence, orange juice and rind. Mix this all very well. Pile the mixture into a lightly floured pudding cloth (a few old threepences or sixpences can be added here if your are lucky enough to have any). Tie the top of the cloth securely and boil for 3 hours. Keep your eye on the boiling water during this time and as it gets low add extra boiling water, being careful to pour it down the sides of the pan and not over the top of the pudding. When cooked cool and hang to store (2 weeks is a good storage time). On the day required, steam the pudding for one hour. Serve with Brandy Custard Sauce with sprigs of holly or small bunches of cherries around it.

ICECREAMLESS

Unbelievable! This is delightful.

1 packet (200 g) creamed coconut

4 cups grape juice, the best you can buy

1 tablespoon lecithin granules

2 teaspoons tahini

2 teaspoons pure vanilla essence

1-2 ripe bananas (optional)

Melt the creamed coconut with 1 cup of the grape juice over a very low heat. Place this, with all of the remaining ingredients in a blender and blend at a high speed for 2 to 3 minutes. Pour into a tray and freeze. Allow it to sit at room temperature for a couple of minutes before serving.

As this is a fairly potent icecream it is really lovely if served with some fruit, such as diced kiwi fruit, sliced bananas, grapes, strawberries, raspberries or fresh peaches. It is also good with a strawberry or peach puree or a fruit sauce. Try adding toasted chopped hazelnuts for something really different.

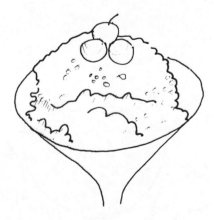

ORANGE AND STRAWBERRY MOUSSE WITH STRAWBERRY COULIS

Gorgeous to look at and gorgeous to eat.

2 punnets strawberries, hulled
1 cup apple juice
1 tablespoon agar-agar
1 cup freshly squeezed and strained orange juice
grated rind from both an orange and a lemon
2 cups ricotta cheese
2 cups natural yoghurt

Select about ½ a punnet of the best strawberries for decoration and puree the remainder. Reserve ½ cup of the puree and chill the remainder to use as the coulis. Heat the apple juice and simmer until reduced by half. Sprinkle the agar-agar over this and simmer for 1 minute until dissolved. Cool a little and stir in the orange juice, orange and lemon rind. Beat the ricotta cheese in a food processor until creamy, blend in the yoghurt and then the ½ cup of strawberry coulis and apple juice mixture. Beat until well combined. Work quickly as the agar-agar can set in no time. Pour the mixture into a dessert mould and chill. To serve, dip the mould up to the rim in hot water for just a few seconds. Invert onto a serving dish. Pour the remaining strawberry puree around the dessert or serve separately in a jug. Decorate the top of the mousse with the remaining strawberries sliced lengthwise.

ORANGE FIESTA WITH VANILLA CREME

An appealing dessert with a difference.

200 g block carob
4 oranges, peeled and thinly sliced, reserve some of the peel to make into thin slivers
3 tablespoons unsweetened pineapple juice
1 1/2 cups ricotta cheese
1 teaspoon honey
1/2 teaspoon vanilla essence
thin slivers of orange peel

Melt the carob in a bowl over hot, but not boiling water. Spread over the back of a baking tray with a spatula. Chill for 10 minutes. Using a long bladed spatula or knife, press the blade away from you across the carob to form long thin curls. Refrigerate. Chill orange pieces. Heat the pineapple juice and simmer until reduced to 1 tablespoonful. Pour over the oranges and chill. Beat the ricotta with the honey and vanilla essence until smooth. Arrange the oranges and juice in 4 serving dishes. Place a heaped spoonful of the ricotta cream on top of each serving and decorate with the carob curls and orange peel.

PERFECTLY PEACHY

A light and creamy dessert just perfect for a hot late summer evening.

6 ripe clingstone peaches
2 cups ricotta cheese or tofu (although tofu can be used, ricotta works best here)
1 cup fruit juice, pear, pineapple or apricot
³⁄₄ tablespoon of agar-agar powder
¹⁄₂ tablespoon of honey, more or less depending on how sweet you like your sweets
grated rind from one orange and one lemon
a pinch of freshly grated nutmeg
a squeeze of lemon juice

Cut the peach flesh and simmer in a little water for about 10 minutes or until the flesh is soft. Cool. Put the ricotta or tofu in a blender and process a little until creamy. Pour the fruit juice into a saucepan, sprinkle the agar-agar powder on top, bring to a simmering point while stirring and stir until dissolved. Cool just a little. Add this, and the remaining ingredients (including the peaches) to the food processor and blend until creamy. Pour into individual serving dishes and chill until set.

As peaches are a delicious late summer fruit, this can be presented with various other delightful fruit combinations. A favourite being Strawberry Sauce. Other serving ideas include — lots of sliced kiwi fruit, very ripe fresh pineapple pieces, fresh ripe peach slices, or banana slices.

PERFECTLY PUMPKIN PIE

For a sweet and oh-so-healthy sensation try this.

PASTRY

This pastry is made without butter or margarine so it will be different, but not difficult to handle
½ cup tofu, ricotta or cottage cheese
2 teaspoons oil (if using tofu)
2 cups wholemeal plain flour
2 tablespoons extra oil
warm water to mix

If using tofu blend the tofu in a food processor with the oil until creamy. Combine the flour with the creamed tofu, ricotta, or cottage cheese. Stir in the oil, and using your hand to mix add sufficient warm water to make a moist, yet firm dough. A little too moist is better than a little too dry. Sprinkle some extra wholemeal flour on a bench top and knead the dough lightly until it is smooth and no longer sticks to your fingers. Roll out and fit it into the pie dish you are using (approx. 22 cm). If the pastry is too soft to be rolled out, don't worry, this is not unusual. All you need to do is put the ball of pastry in the centre of the pie dish and press it out with your fist, gradually working it to fill the pie dish. Trim and neaten the edges.

FILLING

2 cups of tofu, ricotta, or cottage cheese
4 cups of pumpkin puree
½-1 tablespoon honey
¼ teaspoon each nutmeg, cinnamon and ginger
2 tablespoons arrowroot

Blend the tofu in a food processor for ½ to 1 minute on its own. Add all of the remaining ingredients and blend until smooth. Pour into the pastry case and bake in the middle of a moderate oven for 30-35 minutes. Chill.

Serve with Tofu Cream, or Ricotta Cream spread smoothly over the top, or spiked around the edges and decorated with walnut halves, or scattered toasted slivered almonds.

PINEAPPLE AND PASSIONFRUIT CREAM

Different, adventurous, and quite amazing. Give this a try.

2 cups of tofu, ricotta, or a mixture of both
1 teaspoon of oil
½ teaspoon of lemon juice
grated rind of both ½ a lemon and ½ an orange
2 teaspoons of orange juice
flesh from 4-6 passionfruit
2 cups ripe pineapple pieces
1 tablespoon honey
½ cup diced pineapple (extra)

Put the tofu or ricotta in a food processor and blend for ½ a minute. Add the oil and blend for ½ a minute longer. Add all of the remaining ingredients, except the extra diced pineapple, and blend until creamy. Stir in the extra diced pineapple. Pile into a serving dish and refrigerate.

Excellent when served with lots of sliced kiwi fruit, strawberries, or extra passionfruit over the top.

PUMPKIN PIES AND PARADISE

These sweet little pies are certainly enjoyable for an occasional treat.

PASTRY
60 g butter or margarine
1 tablespoon honey
1/4 teaspoon vanilla essence
1 cup wholemeal plain flour

FILLING
1 cup pumpkin puree
1/2 teaspoon mixed spice
1 tablespoon maple syrup
1/2 tablespoon arrowroot
1/3 cup milk or soy milk

TOPPING
2 cups ricotta cheese
2 teaspoons honey
2 drops vanilla essence
walnuts for decoration

To make the pastry, cream the butter and honey together, stir in the vanilla. Add the flour and work into a dough. Chill. Roll out thinly and cut into 8-10 cm circles and fit into muffin pans.

To make the filling combine all of the ingredients together, mixing well. Spoon the filling into the pastry cases and bake in a hot oven (180°C) for 30 minutes. Cool in tins.

To serve beat together the ricotta, honey and essence until smooth. Pipe on top of pumpkin pies and decorate with walnuts.

ROLY-POLY COCONUT BALLS

Worked out by my daughter on one of her cooking sprees, for a snack for her friends. These are great.

2 tablespoons ricotta
1 teaspoon carob powder
1/2-1 cup crushed rice flakes
1/2 cup desiccated coconut

Mix the ricotta with the carob powder then add the crushed rice flakes until the mixture is firm. Form into small balls and roll in coconut. Refrigerate. Fresh flowers on the side of the serving plate look pretty.

STEAMED ORANGE PUDDING

A lovely warm, filling dessert just perfect for a chilly winter's night.

1 tablespoon margarine (you could use a dairy free or soy margarine here)
1/2-1 tablespoon of honey, or a little more if you have a sweet tooth
grated rind and juice of an orange
1 full tablespoon of soy flour
3/4 cup wholemeal self-raising flour
1/2 teaspoon of vanilla essence
soy milk (or cow's milk) to mix

Cream together the margarine and honey, then blend in the orange rind. Sift together the soy flour and wholemeal flour. Fold into the creamed mixture along with the orange juice, vanilla essence and sufficient soy milk to make a moist cake like consistency. Pile into a lightly oiled pudding basin (a 4-5 cup size), cover with 2 thicknesses of foil tied firmly with string. Prepare a large saucepan of boiling water with a rack or steamer in the bottom. Pour hot water, to the depth of about 5 cm into the saucepan, and bring to the boil. Place the pudding in the saucepan and check that the water does not come more than half way up the sides of the pudding basin. Cover the saucepan and let the water bubble gently to cook the pudding. This will take about 1 1/2 hours. Check the water occasionally, and if necessary top up with extra boiling water. Leave the pudding to cool for 5-10 minutes before unmoulding to serve. Decorate with a few overlapping rings of orange on the side.

Try this with a honey flavoured soy custard, or warm soy milk, for a real treat.

STRAWBERRY CREAM

This sweet and lovely dessert cream is easy to prepare and can be served in a variety of ways.

2 cups ricotta cheese, or tofu
2 teaspoons honey
1 cup yoghurt (soy, goat's or cow's)
1 cup strawberries, hulled and washed
1/2 cup toasted almond flakes

Blend the ricotta or tofu until creamy, add the remaining ingredients and blend together thoroughly. Chill.

This can be served as a topping for fresh strawberries or fresh summer fruits, pitted prunes, or dates. It is delicious used as a filling for wholemeal crepes. Roll them up and serve with a sauce of pureed fresh strawberries. Just yum!

STRAWBERRY CREPES

These strawberry crepes add an exotic finish to a meal.

CREPES

¹/₂ cup finely ground wholemeal flour
¹/₂ cup unbleached white flour
1 ¹/₂ cups soy or cow's milk
1 teaspoon oil

FILLING

¹/₂ cup slivered almonds
1 punnet strawberries
1 tablespoon natural strawberry jam sweetened with honey
squeeze of lemon juice
¹/₂ lemon, cut in thin slivers
natural yoghurt

Combine the flours in a bowl, add the milk and oil and beat well to form a thin coating batter. Heat a well oiled crepe pan or small frypan. Pour in sufficient batter to cover the base and cook until golden underneath and dry on top. Turn or flip over and cook a little on the other side. Turn onto a plate. Make more crepes stacking them on top of each other. Any extra can be frozen.

To make the filling, toast the almonds on a dry baking tray in the oven until golden. Cut the strawberries in half, leaving a few whole for decorating. Heat the jam and add the strawberries and lemon juice, stir for 1 minute. Place a spoonful of strawberries on half a crepe, fold over and fill the number required. Sprinkle with the toasted almonds and decorate with lemon slices and whole strawberries. Serve with a dollop of natural yoghurt on the side. The toasted almonds may be mixed with the strawberry filling.

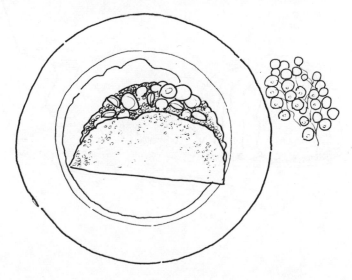

STRAWBERRY YOGHURT ICECREAM

So healthy and so delicious.

3 cups yoghurt (approx. 750 ml).

1 cup strawberries, chopped

1 tablespoon sunflower seeds

½-1 tablespoon honey

grated rind of 1 orange, or 1 lemon

2 tablespoons sultanas, raisins or chopped dried apricots soaked in 1 tablespoon of fruit juice (optional)

Combine all of these ingredients and mix carefully. Freeze for 2 to 3 hours. Allow to stand at room temperature for 5 minutes before serving. Toasted chopped hazelnuts also make a lovely addition.

This icecream is best when served on its own.

SUMMER PUDDING

Suntans, surf, sparkles on the water, long lazy days, heaps of salads and summer pudding.

8-10 slices of stale wholemeal bread, crusts removed
1/2-1 tablespoon honey, as desired
125 ml water
750 g firm fresh berries, such as raspberries, blackberries, red currants
juice of 1 orange
a little grated orange rind
1 cup ricotta cheese
1 teaspoon honey
1/4 teaspoon vanilla essence
extra blackberries for decoration

Cut a circle from one slice of bread to fit the base of a 1 litre pudding basin. Cut bread into fingers and arrange around the sides of the basin avoiding any gaps. Bring honey and water to simmering point in a large saucepan. Add fruit and shake pan from side to side until all fruit is submerged and liquid has returned to simmering point. Remove from heat and strain fruit, reserving syrup. Add orange juice and rind to the syrup and spoon enough syrup over the bread to soak thoroughly and evenly. Spoon drained fruit over bread. Arrange more bread on top and spoon over a little more syrup. Cover with plastic wrap and place a saucer on top. Weigh down with something around 1 kg in weight and refrigerate for a day. Unmould pudding onto a serving dish and spoon remaining syrup over. Beat the ricotta cheese with the honey and vanilla essence. Pipe around the edge of the pudding and decorate with the extra berries. Cut into wedges to serve.

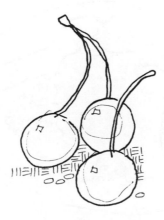

SUPER DOOPER COCONUT PIES

A healthy fun dessert made by my daughter. The children will love to try this one.

PASTRY

1 cup wholemeal plain flour

½ tablespoon margarine

a little warm water as needed

Place the flour in a bowl and rub the margarine in using fingertips until the mixture resembles breadcrumbs. Add sufficient warm water until you have a soft scone dough. Lift the dough out onto a well floured bench and knead lightly until it is smooth and not sticky. Roll out making sure there is always enough flour underneath, and cut shapes to fit small pie foils or patty tins. Fit the pastry into the shapes, leaving some for the top.

FILLING

½ cup blackberry jam sweetened with honey

1 cup desiccated coconut

1 cup ricotta cheese

1 cup crushed rice flakes

Place a teaspoon of jam in the base of each pastry shell. Sprinkle this with a little coconut, cover with a spoonful of ricotta cheese and sprinkle with the rice flakes. Roll out the remaining pastry and cut into strips approximately 1 cm wide. Lattice these over the top of each pie, sealing the edges with a little water. Bake in a hot oven (200°C) for 12 to 15 minutes. These are great.

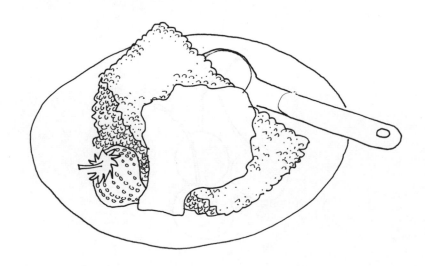

SWEET STRUDEL SURPRISE

For something different, this is worth the effort.

6 sheets filo pastry
oil
1 cup walnuts, very finely chopped
1 1/2 cups ricotta cheese, or pureed tofu
2 teaspoons honey
2 cups sliced peaches or apricots lightly cooked in a little water
1/2 cup chopped raisins
a little cinnamon
1 tablespoon extra chopped walnuts

Lay 2 pastry sheets on a bench on top of each other and brush lightly with the oil. Sprinkle 2 tablespoons of the walnuts evenly over them. Repeat this using the remaining 4 sheets of pastry, placing them directly on top of each other and using all of the walnuts. Combine the ricotta or tofu and honey together mixing well. Spread this along the longest edge of the pastry about 10 cm in from the edge. Cover evenly with the peaches and raisins, then dust a little cinnamon over the top. Fold the 10 cm edge over the filling, tuck in the ends then carefully roll to completely enclose the filling, keeping the join underneath. Lift onto a large well oiled oven tray. Brush with a little oil and sprinkle with walnuts. Bake in a moderate oven for 25 minutes until crisp and brown. Serve hot or cold. Superb!

VERY FRUITY FRUIT BALLS

For a simple little after dinner treat or anytime snack, try these tasty powerful little balls of goodness.

1 cup dates, very finely chopped
1 cup prunes, very finely chopped
2 cups raisins, finely chopped
1 tablespoon sesame seeds
juice of half an orange
½ teaspoon grated orange rind
½ cup desiccated coconut
1 ripe banana, mashed
squeeze of lemon juice

Combine all of these ingredients together mixing very well. Using your hands roll into small balls about the size of a walnut. Add an extra banana or some yoghurt if the mixture is too dry. Chill. Unless you are tempted these will keep refrigerated for up to 2 weeks.

To dress them up a little, try pressing half a grape or almond on the top of each, or roll them in extra desiccated coconut or serve them on a colourful platter of fresh fruit.

VERY FRUITY ICECREAM

Easy to make, tastes great, and is good for you. What more can you ask for?

2 ripe bananas
juice of half a lemon
1 cup of yoghurt (any type)
½ cup unsweetened pineapple juice
1 cup strawberries, or fresh peach slices

Peel the bananas, dip in lemon juice, wrap in plastic and freeze until firm. Slice the frozen banana and place in the blender with the yoghurt, pineapple juice, and strawberries, or peaches. Blend until creamy. Pour into a container and freeze. Allow to stand at room temperature for 5 minutes before serving.

Just great served with any sliced fruit, strawberries or raspberries.

Dressings, sauces and spreads

BRANDY CUSTARD SAUCE

2 tablespoons maize cornflour
a little cold water
2 cups soy milk, or cow's milk
2 teaspoons of honey
1 tablespoon brandy
1/2 teaspoon vanilla essence

Blend the cornflour with a little cold water to dissolve. Stir in the soy milk, honey and brandy. Bring to the boil while stirring and simmer for one minute. Stir in the vanilla essence and serve while warm.

CORN 'N TOFU CREAM SAUCE

I remember enjoying a parsley white sauce when I was little. Here's an old fashioned recipe with a twist.

3 cobs of corn, or equivalent to 2 cups of corn
250 g tofu, cut in cubes
2 teaspoons tamari
2 tablespoons cornflour
a little cold water
1 cup of soy milk
1 cup of water
1 tablespoon chopped parsley
black pepper

Prepare the cobs of corn by steaming the corn for 10 minutes, and then cutting off the kernels. Put the tofu cubes in a bowl and sprinkle with the tamari. Dissolve the cornflour in the cold water and pour into a saucepan along with the soy milk and water. Bring to boil over a moderate heat while stirring. Add the parsley, pepper, corn, tofu, and remaining tamari. Heat through and check the seasonings before serving. Some sliced mushrooms or steamed green peas could be added with the corn.

Surprisingly simple to make, this recipe can form the basis of a meal when served with pumpkin and potato mashed together, or brown rice and a fresh vegetable and sprout salad. Tomato wedges on the plate add colour.

CREAMED ASPARAGUS SPREAD

Make the most of asparagus when it's in season with this pleasing spread.

2 cups asparagus pieces
1 cup ricotta cheese or mashed tofu
juice of a lemon
1 teaspoon tamari
pinch each of dill and cayenne
black pepper

Steam the asparagus until quite tender. Drain well. Blend the ricotta or tofu in a food processor until creamy. Add the asparagus with the remaining ingredients and blend until smooth. Chill.

CURRIED SESAME SPREAD

Delicious on hot wholemeal toast or muffins, or try it as a dip with crunchy celery pieces.

¹/₂ cup sesame seeds
2 cups tofu, ricotta or cottage cheese
1 tomato, chopped and drained
1 teaspoon tamari
1 teaspoon curry powder
¹/₂ teaspoon tumeric
1 tablespoon yoghurt, soy yoghurt can be used
1 tablespoon tahini (optional)
1 tablespoon unsweetened tomato chutney (optional)
1 teaspoon lemon juice

Place the sesame seeds on a dry baking tray and toast in a moderate oven for 8-10 minutes or until golden. Combine all the remaining ingredients and blend until smooth. Stir in the sesame seeds and serve.

Some finely sliced spring onion can be added for extra zing.

FRESH TOMATO SAUCE

500 g tomatoes, chopped
1 onion, finely chopped
1 clove garlic, crushed
¹/₂ teaspoon honey
2 teaspoons cider vinegar
a little fresh or dried thyme
vegetable salt
white pepper

Combine all of these ingredients in a saucepan, bring to the boil and simmer uncovered for 30 minutes. Puree the sauce through a sieve and refrigerate until ready to use.

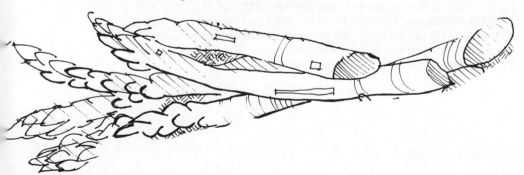

HERB SAUCE

1 cup natural yoghurt (you can use soy, goat or cow's
milk yoghurt)

1 tablespoon each cider vinegar and lemon juice

1 teaspoon mustard mixed with a little water

$^{1}/_{4}$ teaspoon each fennel and carraway seed

$^{1}/_{2}$ teaspoon dill seed, or 2 teaspoons fresh dill

$^{1}/_{4}$ teaspoon vegetable salt

black pepper

$^{1}/_{3}$ cup oil

These ingredients can be blended together in a food processor, or
stirred in a bowl adding the oil a little at a time. Serve well chilled.

MUSHROOM NOODLE SAUCE

*Wholemeal pasta provides fibre and complex carbohydrates which are
important in our diet.*

1 tablespoon water

2 leeks thinly sliced

1 onion, in half rings

2 cups thinly sliced mushrooms

1 cup broccoli cut in small flowers

4 tomatoes, finely chopped

$^{1}/_{2}$ tablespoon oil

$1^{1}/_{2}$ tablespoons finely ground wholemeal flour or
unbleached white flour

$1^{1}/_{2}$ cups water

2 teaspoons tamari

1 tablespoon chopped parsley

1 cup tofu cubes

Heat the water in saucepan and cook the leeks and onions for 3
minutes, add the mushrooms, broccoli and tomatoes, stir and cook
for 5 minutes. In a separate saucepan blend the oil and flour and
heat for 3 minutes. Remove from the heat and blend in the water,
reheat and stir until it boils, stir in the tamari and parsley. Combine
the sauce with the vegetables and simmer for 3-5 minutes. Stir in
the tofu and serve over hot wholemeal pasta.

PEANUT SPREAD

Delicious as a spread or dip, or rolled in lettuce or cabbage leaves as a salad or snack.

$1/2$ cup pure peanut butter
1 cup of mashed tofu or ricotta cheese
2 teaspoons of homemade tomato chutney
1 teaspoon lemon juice
a little tamari if needed
black pepper

Combine and blend all of these ingredients together. Serve with biscuits, or celery and carrot sticks. Keeps refrigerated for up to 5 days if not used immediately.

RICOTTA CREAM

Ricotta, when beaten has a lovely light thick cream consistency, just perfect for cakes. It can actually be piped.

2 cups ricotta cheese
$1/2$ tablespoon of honey
$1/2$ teaspoon of vanilla essence

Start to beat the ricotta in a food processor, then add the honey and vanilla essence. Beat for about one minute. Can be used immediately or refrigerated for 2 days.

SESAME AND SWEET SANDWICH SPREAD

This is certainly something different.

$^1/_3$ cup toasted sesame seeds

1 cup ricotta cheese, or pureed tofu

1 teaspoon tahini (optional)

1-2 teaspoons honey, or more for the sweet tooth

$^1/_2$ cup thinly sliced celery

$^1/_2$ cup chopped dates **or** chopped raisins **or** sliced banana **or** sultanas

Blend together the sesame seeds, ricotta or tofu, tahini and honey and beat until smooth. Spread on fresh or toasted wholegrain bread, top with the celery, and the dates, raisins, banana, or sultanas.

STRAWBERRY SAUCE

1 punnet of strawberries

$^1/_4$ cup water

1 teaspoon of honey if desired

squeeze of lemon juice

Chop the strawberries and cook for 3-5 minutes with the remaining ingredients. Stir well so it becomes thick and mushy. A little extra water can be added, or the sauce can be thickened with a teaspoon of kuzu or arrowroot dissolved in a little water, if desired.

SWEET ALMOND CREAM

A wonderfully healthy cream, perfect to dollop on desserts.

1 cup blanched almonds

$^1/_2$ cup apple juice

1 cup ricotta cheese or tofu

juice and grated rind of $^1/_2$ a lemon

$^1/_2$ teaspoon pure vanilla essence

Put the almonds in a food processor and blend until very fine, then slowly add the apple juice to make a thick paste. Add the remaining ingredients and blend until creamy. Serve chilled.

SWEET BANANA TREAT

Liven up your morning muesli or dollop over fruit desserts, this adds sweetness, flavour and plenty of zap.

2 ripe bananas

1/2 cup sunflower seeds

2 tablespoons natural yoghurt

pinch of nutmeg

squeeze of lemon juice (optional)

Combine all the ingredients in a food processor and blend until smooth. Serve at once or chill.

TANGY TOFU SPREAD

Excellent on rye toast, great in salad sandwiches, tasty as a dip, and just amazing dolloped on top of hot roast potatoes.

2 cups tofu (ricotta or cottage cheese can be used)

juice of 1/2 a lemon

2 teaspoons tamari

1/2 teaspoon curry powder

1/4 teaspoon each tumeric and dry mustard

1 clove crushed garlic

1/2 cup chopped, drained tomato (optional)

Break up the tofu and blend it in a food processor until smooth. Add all of the remaining ingredients and process well. Serve or refrigerate until needed.

TOFU CREAM

This is deliciously healthy and makes enough to spread over one cake.

1 cup of tofu
2 teaspoons honey
½ teaspoon of pure vanilla essence
½ teaspoon grated lemon rind (or orange rind)
2 teaspoons of tahini if desired

Blend all of these ingredients together, in a food processor until smooth.

TOFU MAYONNAISE

This tangy mayonnaise always surprises me by its popularity. Vegetable salt is used here instead of tamari, to maintain a pale, creamy colour.

1 cup of tofu
¼ cup of lemon juice and cider vinegar mixed
¼ to ½ teaspoon of vegetable salt
½ teaspoon dry mustard
1 teaspoon honey
¼ cup oil

Blend the tofu for one minute on its own in a food processor to allow it to break down a little. Add all of the remaining ingredients and blend until smooth. Chill before serving. Serve with a little grated nutmeg on top.

This goes really well with any vegetable salad, or burgers.

TOMATO AND PUMPKIN SAUCE

A little unusual but really lovely.

2 teaspoons oil or water
2 onions, diced
1-2 cloves of garlic
2 teaspoons grated fresh ginger, or ½ teaspoon powdered ginger
6 tomatoes, chopped
2 cups diced pumpkin
juice of half a lemon
½ teaspoon oregano
½ teaspoon basil
1 cup water
2 teaspoons light coloured miso — optional
2 teaspoons tamari

Heat the oil or water in a large saucepan and cook the onions, garlic and ginger for 2 to 3 minutes. Add the tomatoes, pumpkin, lemon juice, oregano, basil and water. Cover and simmer for 15 to 20 minutes or until the pumpkin is soft. Mash with a potato masher or puree in a food processor until smooth. Stir in the tamari, reheat and serve.

This is a wonderful sauce to serve over lightly steamed vegetables with brown rice, or with vegetable patties.

WHITE SAUCE

A well flavoured sauce that is ideal to serve with many vegetarian main dishes.

1 tablespoon oil
1 onion diced
1 clove crushed garlic
½ cup finely ground wholemeal flour, or unbleached white flour
1½ cups water or milk
2 teaspoons tamari or soy sauce
1 teaspoon dried basil
½ cup chopped parsley
¼ cup tahini (optional)

Heat the oil and lightly fry the onion and garlic for 3-4 minutes, stir in the flour and cook 2 minutes. Remove and stir in the liquid. Bring to the boil while stirring then add the remaining ingredients. Reheat and it's ready to use.

ZUCCHINI AND GARLIC SPREAD

Full of flavour and totally delectable this goes well as a dip or as a picnic spread with crusty fresh wholemeal rolls.

5 medium zucchini, sliced
2 medium eggplants, sliced
8 ripe tomatoes, chopped
2 cloves garlic, crushed
1 teaspoon tamari
black pepper
pinch of cayenne
1 tablespoon tahini (optional)

Steam the zucchini and eggplant until quite tender. Dry fry the tomatoes and garlic until mushy. Blend all of the ingredients together in a food processor. Serve hot or cold.

Cakes and cookies

BANANA BUNS

Wholesome and tasty these buns are enticing when served hot with butter after a light lunch.

1 sachet dried yeast

$^1/_2$ cup lukewarm water

$^1/_2$ teaspoon honey

3 ripe bananas

1 tablespoon each prunes and raisins, chopped

$^1/_2$ cup yoghurt

1 tablespoon lemon juice

$^1/_2$ teaspoon vanilla

a little grated fresh nutmeg

1$^1/_2$ cups each unbleached white flour and wholemeal plain flour

Dissolve the yeast in the warm water and stir in the honey. Leave in a warm place for 5 minutes until the mixture is frothy. Meanwhile mash the bananas and stir in the prunes, raisins, yoghurt, lemon juice, vanilla and nutmeg. Sift the flours together. Stir 1 cup of flour into the banana mixture. Add the yeast with the remaining flour mixing well. The dough should be a little sticky but not too wet. Pile spoonfuls onto a lightly oiled baking tray and leave in a warm place to rise from 15-20 minutes. Bake in a hot oven at 180°C for 20 minutes or until buns are golden.

BANANA, ZUCCHINI AND CARROT CAKE

You can have cake, and good health too.

2 cups wholemeal plain flour
1 teaspoon bicarbonate of soda
2 cups wholemeal self-raising flour can be used instead

1 teaspoon ground cinnamon

1/2 cup chopped walnuts

1/2 cup honey

2/3 cup vegetable oil

2 mashed ripe bananas

3/4 cup each grated zucchini and carrot

Sift together the flour, soda and cinnamon. Stir in the walnuts. Beat the honey, oil and bananas together until smooth. Combine the flour mixture, honey mixture and zucchini and carrots. Stir until well blended. Add a little soy milk or water if the mixture is too dry. Spoon into a well oiled loaf tin (approximately 22 cm). Bake at 180°C for 35-40 minutes or until golden and firm.

BUCKWHEAT MUFFINS

These muffins can be made suitable for a wheat-free, dairy-free or low fat diet. Try them hot from the oven with a fruit puree jam.

1/2 tablespoon active dry yeast

1 1/4 cups lukewarm water

1 teaspoon honey

1 cup buckwheat flour

1 1/2 cups wholemeal, rye, or barley flour

1/2 cup yoghurt (cow's, goat's, or soy milk yoghurt)

1 tablespoon tahini or ground sunflower seeds

pinch of cinnamon

Making sure that the water is not too hot, as it would kill the yeast, combine the yeast, water and honey. Leave in a warm place for 5 minutes until frothy. Put the remaining ingredients into a bowl and stir in the yeast mixture. Lightly oil a muffin tray and dust with flour. Fill with the muffin mixture. Place the tray in a warm place for 15 minutes to allow the muffins to begin to rise. Cook in a hot oven at 200°C for 25-30 minutes.

CAROB ORANGE CAKE

Carob seems to live in the shadow of chocolate, which is unfair as carob is delicious in its own right, especially when paired with orange. In this moist cake, carob buds go into the cake mix as well as on top.

1/2 cup butter or margarine
1 tablespoon honey
1 teaspoon vanilla essence
grated rind of 1 orange
1 cup each wholemeal self-raising flour and unbleached white flour
1-2 cups buttermilk
1 cup chopped carob buds
FOR THE TOP
1/2 cup carob buds and 1/2 cup chopped walnuts

Cream together the butter and honey with the vanilla essence and orange rind. Sift together the flours and add to the butter mixture along with the buttermilk. Stir carefully to make a moist dough. Stir in the carob buds. Pour into a lightly oiled 20-22 cm cake pan. Combine the remaining carob buds with the walnuts and scatter them over the cake mixture. Bake in a moderate oven for 35-45 minutes.

CARROT AND CASHEW CAKE

Another low fat unsweetened cake that is always handy to have.

1 1/2 cups wholemeal self-raising flour or a mixture of brown rice flour and ground oats
1/2 tablespoon cinnamon
1/2 cup arrowroot or soy flour
1/2 cup chopped cashews
2 cups grated carrots
1/2 teaspoon pure vanilla essence
1 cup fruit juice or carrot juice
1/3 cup tahini

Sift the flour, cinnamon and arrowroot. Combine together the cashews and carrots, and stir this into the flour along with the vanilla, juice and tahini. Spoon into a lightly oiled and floured loaf tin and bake at 175°C for 45 minutes. Cover while cooling.

CARROT CAKE

Simple, tasty, and always popular.

¼-½ cup honey
½ cup vegetable oil
3 cups grated carrot
1½ cups wholemeal self-raising flour
½ teaspoon each baking powder, bicarb soda, nutmeg and cinnamon
1 cup ricotta cheese
2 teaspoons honey
½ teaspoon vanilla essence
a little extra grated nutmeg

Blend together the honey and oil, stir in the carrots. Sift together the flour, baking powder, soda, nutmeg, and cinnamon. Combine the flour and honey mixtures together. Spoon into a well oiled loaf tin (approximately 22 cm long) and bake in a moderate oven (180°C) until golden and firm for approximately 35-40 minutes. Cool. Beat together the ricotta cheese, honey and vanilla essence in a food processor. Spread thickly over the top of the cake, dust with a little extra nutmeg and serve.

CARROT MUFFINS

These golden coloured unsweetened carrot muffins are like a savoury bun to have with piping hot soup for a wintery Sunday lunch.

2 cups finely grated carrots
2½ cups wholemeal self-raising flour
½ cup soy flour
½ cup tahini
1 cup yoghurt (cow's, goat's or soy milk yoghurt, or pureed tofu)
1 cup cow's milk, soy milk, or carrot juice

Combine all of the ingredients, mixing well. Spoon into a lightly oiled and floured muffin tin, and bake at 175°C for 45 minutes. Serve hot.

CRUNCHY SESAME SULTANA COOKIES

Specially made without any sugars, wheat flour, or dairy products to suit allergy sufferers, or simply to add plenty of variety to our diet.

½ cup chopped dates
¼ cup apple juice, or water
2 ripe bananas
1 green apple, grated
juice of ½ a lemon
1 cup oats
½ cup sultanas
½ cup sesame seeds
½ cup rice flour
pinch of cinnamon

Simmer the dates in the apple juice or water for 5 minutes. Mash the bananas and combine with the grated apple and lemon juice. Stir in the dates, sultanas, sesame seeds, oats, rice flour and cinnamon. Mix well. Place spoonfuls on a lightly oiled baking tray and bake in a moderate oven for 15 minutes. Cover while cooling.

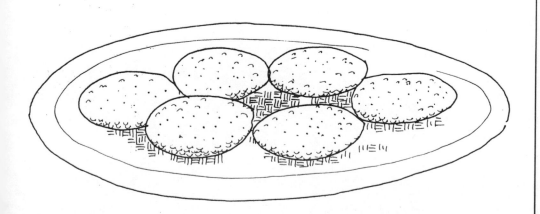

CURRANT AND SUNFLOWER SLICE

A sugar-free recipe, full of goodies and ideal for after school snacks.

PASTRY

1½ cups wholemeal plain flour
1½ cups rolled oats
½ cup coconut
½ cup oil
1 cup water

TOPPING

1½ cups currants
juice of a lemon
1¼ cups water
3 tablespoons arrowroot or kuzu dissolved in 3 tablespoons water
2 tablespoons sunflower seeds
1 tablespoon coconut

Make the pastry by combining the flour, oats and coconut. Mix in the oil and water and stir well. Press into a lightly oiled shallow baking tray and bake at 200°C for 20-30 minutes. Combine the currants, lemon juice and water. Bring to the boil and simmer 8-10 minutes. Blend the arrowroot with the water, add to the currants and stir until thick. Spread the fruit mixture over the pastry, sprinkle with sunflower seeds and coconut. Chill. Cut into squares.

DATE AND OAT MOUNTAINS

For all those with food intolerances to wheat or dairy products, or who are on a low fat or sugar-free diet, these are just what the doctor ordered!

2 ripe bananas
1 grated apple
squeeze of lemon juice
1/2 cup chopped dates
1/2 cup water
1/2 cup each sultanas and sesame seeds
1/2 cup cornmeal or pure cornflour
1 cup rolled oats
1/2 cup rice flour
pinch of cinnamon

Mash the bananas in a bowl, combine with the grated apple and stir in the lemon juice. Cook the dates in the water for about 5 minutes or until quite soft. Combine with all of the remaining ingredients including the banana mixture. Stir well. Put spoonfuls on a lightly oiled baking tray and bake in a moderate oven (170°C) for 12-15 minutes. Cover with a tea-towel while cooling to prevent them drying out.

DATE AND RAISIN CHEWS

Full of dates and raisins, this rich, moist slice needs no extra sweetening.

10 dates, chopped
1/3 cup water
1/2 cup raisins, chopped
1 cup wholemeal self-raising flour
1 tablespoon oil or tahini
1/2 cup walnuts, chopped
1 teaspoon pure vanilla essence
4 tablespoons milk or soy milk

Put the dates and water in a saucepan, bring to the boil and simmer 10 minutes. Beat with a wooden spoon until smooth. Mix in the raisins, flour, oil or tahini, walnuts, vanilla and milk, combining well. Spread evenly into a greased shallow baking tin. Bake for 25-30 minutes at 180°C. Cut into finger lengths when cool.

FRESH FRUIT CAKE

2 cups rolled oats

2½ cups wholemeal self-raising flour

1 cup chopped nuts

½ cup shredded coconut

1 teaspoon cinnamon

1 cup each raisins and dried apricots, chopped

3 cups fruit juice

½ cup oil

grated rind from one orange

1 teaspoon vanilla essence

3 ripe bananas

squeezed lemon juice

Lightly toast the rolled oats on a dry baking tray. Combine the rolled oats, flour, nuts, coconut and cinnamon. Mix the raisins and apricots with the fruit juice, oil, orange rind and vanilla — let stand for ½ hour. Mash the bananas and add the lemon juice.

Combine all of the ingredients together, mixing well. Spoon into a lightly oiled loaf pan and bake at 160°C for 40-50 minutes or until cooked.

FRUIT RING CAKE

A very moist and tasty cake.

2 cups chopped peaches or apricots

1 cup dried fruit, sultanas, raisins and currants

½ cup each orange juice and apricot nectar

1 tablespoon honey

2 cups wholemeal plain flour
2 teaspoons baking powder
(2 cups wholemeal self-raising flour can be used instead)

½ cup coconut

¾ cup rolled oats

Cook the peaches or apricots in a little water until soft. Add the dried fruits, orange juice, apricot nectar and honey. Allow to cool. Sift the flour with the baking powder, and add to the fruit with all the remaining ingredients. Mix well. Add a little extra juice if it is too dry. Place in a greased ring tin and sprinkle sunflower or sesame seeds on top. Bake in a moderate oven (180°C) for 35-45 minutes. Cool and serve sliced and buttered.

MOIST FRUIT AND PUMPKIN CAKE

Naturally sweetened this fruit cake is delicious.

125 g each sultanas, raisins and chopped dried apricots
1½ cups apple juice
1 teaspoon bicarbonate of soda
1 cup mashed pumpkin
1 cup grated carrot
250 g wholemeal self-raising flour
1 teaspoon mixed spice
½ cup yoghurt or 2 mashed ripe bananas

Put the dried fruits, and apple juice into a saucepan. Bring to the boil. Add the bicarbonate of soda and take care as it will froth up. Cool a little. Combine the mashed pumpkin, grated carrot, flour and spice. Add the dried fruit mixture and stir well adding sufficient yoghurt or mashed bananas to make a moist mixture of a dropping consistency. Well oil and line a 20 cm tin and pile the cake mixture in. Bake in a moderate oven 180°C for 40-50 minutes or until cooked. Cool in the tin for 10 minutes before turning out.

NUTTY COCONUT SULTANA SLICE

An excellent and nutritious snack.

2 cups wholemeal plain flour
1 tablespoon soy flour
1 cup desiccated coconut
½-1 tablespoon honey
¾ cup sultanas
½ cup chopped walnuts
½ cup oil
½-1 cup soy milk, or fresh orange juice

Mix all of the ingredients together and press into an oiled lamington tin. Bake in a moderate oven at 190°C for 25 minutes, or until golden brown. Cool in the tray. Cut into bars while still warm.

PEANUT BUTTER COOKIES

These are so tasty, they make a great snack any time.

½ cup peanut butter
1 ½ cups wholemeal self-raising flour
2 tablespoons oil
1 tablespoon tahini
1 tablespoon honey
grated rind and juice of an orange
1 teaspoon vanilla essence
½ cup peanuts

Combine all of the ingredients together, mixing well. Roll the mixture into walnut sized balls, place on a well oiled baking tray and flatten a little with a fork. Bake in a moderately hot oven (200°C) for 15 minutes or until golden brown.

PUMPKIN COOKIES

If they don't like pumpkin for dinner, try it in these cakes.

125 g margarine
¼-½ cup honey
½ cup mashed pumpkin
¼ teaspoon pure vanilla essence
1 cup wholemeal self-raising flour
½ teaspoon cinnamon
pinch of ground nutmeg
½ cup sultanas
¼ cup chopped walnuts

Cream together the margarine and honey. Stir in the pumpkin and vanilla. Sift the flour and spices, then add this to the creamed mixture. Add the sultanas and nuts. Drop small spoonfuls onto an oiled tray and bake in a moderate oven (200°C) for 8 to 10 minutes. Cool.

SESAME SEED HOT CAKES

These Chinese hot-cakes are traditionally served with a vegetable hot-pot. The rest of the meal will need to be organised so these can be served as soon as they are cooked.

250 g wholemeal plain flour
1 teaspoon honey
½ teaspoon vegetable salt
½ teaspoon baking powder
2 teaspoons sesame oil
½ cup water, or more if needed
½ cup sesame seeds

Combine the flour, honey, salt and baking powder in a mixing bowl. Add the sesame oil and water and mix to make a smooth dough. Turn the dough on to a lightly floured bench and knead it for 5 minutes. Shape the dough into a long sausage roll, about 5 cm in diameter. Cut the roll into 5 cm pieces. Pat each piece into a ball and flatten each into a cake about 1 cm thick. Moisten one side of each cake with a little cold water and press the wet side into the sesame seeds to coat it thoroughly. Heat a large frying pan over a moderate heat and lightly brush with oil. Cook the cakes for 5 minutes, sesame coated sides uppermost. Arrange the cakes on a baking tray, still with sesame seeds uppermost, and grill for 4 to 5 minutes or until the sesame seeds become golden. Serve the cakes hot.

SPICY APPLE CAKE

This cake can be made as a loaf or into small cakes and is sweetened naturally with the fruits. No fats are used.

½ cup sultanas
¾ cup apple juice
1½ cups wholemeal self-raising flour
½ cup soy flour
1 teaspoon cinnamon
½ teaspoon nutmeg
1½ cups grated green apples

Soak the sultanas in the apple juice for half an hour or longer. Sift together the flours, cinnamon and nutmeg. Combine the sultanas and juice, flours and grated apples, adding a little extra apple juice if it is too dry. Spoon into an oiled and lightly floured loaf tin and bake at 175°C for 50-60 minutes. Small cakes are baked for 30 minutes. Cover while cooling.

TOTALLY HEALTHY FRUIT CAKE

This amazing fruit cake recipe come with thanks to my wonderful sister Sandie, with memories of the great times we have together.

100 g dried apricots
75 g dried apple
125 g each prunes, dates, currants and sultanas
200 g raisins
$1/2$ cup unsweetened pineapple juice
$1/2$ cup water
juice of 2 oranges
grated rind of an orange
$1 1/2$ cups natural yoghurt
$1/4$ cup cornmeal
$2 1/2$ cups wholemeal self-raising flour
$1/2$ cup rolled oats
$1/2$ teaspoon each nutmeg and cinnamon

Roughly chop the apricots, dried apple, prunes and dates, and combine this with the other fruits. Pour the pineapple juice, water and orange juice over the fruit, mix well and leave to soak for several hours, turning occasionally. Stir in the orange rind and yoghurt. Add the cornmeal, sifted flour, oats and spices. Mix thoroughly. Divide the mixture into two 20 cm round cake tins which have been lightly oiled, or lined with non-stick baking paper. Sprinkle a little cold water on the top and bake in a slow to moderate oven for $1 1/4$ to $1 1/2$ hours or until cooked when tested with a skewer. Cool.

As this cake does not have any fat or sweetening in it to help its keeping qualities, it will need to be kept refrigerated either wrapped in foil, or in an airtight container.

WHOLEMEAL HONEY APPLE ROUND

A moist and tasty apple cake. Just right for afternoon tea, or as a pudding.

1¾ cups wholemeal self-raising flour

1 teaspoon ground cinnamon

¼ teaspoon grated nutmeg

2 medium green apples, peeled and diced finely

90 g margarine (a dairy-free margarine can be used)

¼-½ cup honey

¾ cup natural yoghurt (goat's, soy, or cow's milk yoghurt can be used)

1 extra apple, peeled, cored and cut into thin wedges

cinnamon

½ tablespoon honey, warmed

Sift the flour, cinnamon and nutmeg together. Stir in the diced apples. Beat the margarine and honey together until light. Add the flour mixture alternately with the yoghurt. Stir well until combined, adding a little extra yoghurt if the mixture is too dry. Spoon the mixture into a well oiled 23 cm springform tin. Dust the apple wedges with the cinnamon and push them into the cake mixture in a spoke fashion. Bake in a moderate oven (180°C gas/200°C elec) for about 45-50 minutes or until cooked. Brush with warm honey while still hot, and remove from the tin when a little cooled.

ZUCCHINI AND WALNUT CAKE

More of a loaf than a cake, this is low in fat and has a lovely crunchy crust. The wholemeal flour can be replaced with another grain, but it will be a heavier loaf.

1 cup wholemeal self-raising flour, rye flour, millet flour or brown rice flour
½ cup soy flour
1 teaspoon cinnamon
¾ cup finely chopped or ground walnuts
1½ cups finely grated zucchini
½ cup pureed tofu or yoghurt
⅓-½ cup apple juice

Sift together the flours and cinnamon. Combine the walnuts, zucchini, tofu and apple juice. Add to the flour and mix well. Pile into a lightly oiled and floured loaf tin and bake at 160°C for 30-40 minutes or until cooked when tested. Cover while cooling. Serve sliced.

Also . . .

BERRY GOOD JAM

Just excellent, this leaves the sugar laden jam miles behind.

3 cups fresh apricots, chopped
2 cups blackberries or raspberries
2 tablespoons arrowroot or kuzu
a little cold water
squeeze of lemon juice

Cook the apricots in a little water until soft. Blend the berries into a puree. Dissolve the arrowroot in a little cold water and lemon juice. Put all of the ingredients in a food processor and blend until smooth. Heat and stir briskly until it thickens. Cool and refrigerate in airtight jars.

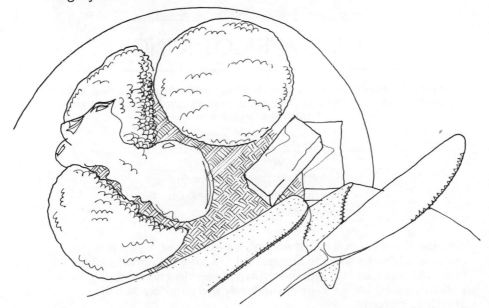

CHRISTMAS CHEER

6 oranges

2 ripe bananas

5 mint leaves

850 ml unsweetened pineapple juice

750 ml bottle mineral water

1 cup pure grape juice

10 strawberries

ice

Reserve one orange. Juice the remaining 5 oranges and blend with the bananas and mint leaves in a blender. Combine with all remaining ingredients, except the strawberries and ice. Chill thoroughly. Garnish glasses with the strawberries and orange slices, and serve the drink over ice with a sprig of mint.

DRIED APRICOT ICING

This is a bright colourful icing with a tang from the orange rind. Other dried fruits such as dates, raisins, or prunes can be used for a rich looking brown icing.

2 cups dried apricots, chopped

water to cover

1/2 teaspoon grated orange rind

1 tablespoon arrowroot or kuzu

1/2 cup shredded coconut, lightly toasted

Simmer the dried fruit in just enough water to cover. When soft puree in a blender with the orange rind. Dissolve the arrowroot in a little cold water and stir into the apricot puree. Heat while stirring until thickened. Ice the cake immediately and decorate with the shredded coconut.

DRIED FRUIT JAM

A tasty healthy jam that needs to be kept refrigerated.

4 cups fresh fruit in season, chopped

1 cup chopped dates or sultanas

1 teaspoon lemon juice

*1 tablespoon arrowroot or kuzu (optional) dissolved in
1 tablespoon cold water*

Simmer the fresh fruit in a little water until quite soft. Add the dried fruits and lemon juice and simmer a further 8-10 minutes, adding a little extra water if necessary. Blend in a food processor until smooth. Dissolve the arrowroot in the cold water, stir it into the fruits and reheat while stirring until thickened. Cool and store in an airtight jar in the refrigerator.

FRUIT PORRIDGE

A great way to warm up on a cold morning.

1 cup rolled oats

2¹/₂ cups water

*²/₃ cup chopped mixed dried fruit; for example, apricots,
sultanas, raisins and dates*

¹/₂ tablespoon sunflower seeds

cinnamon

soy milk (or cow's milk)

Place rolled oats and water in a large saucepan. Bring to the boil, lower the heat and simmer for 15 minutes or until the porridge is thick. Add the dried fruit and sunflower seeds and cook for a further 2 to 3 minutes. Serve with cinnamon and soy milk.

INDIAN PARATHAS

A delightful flaky Indian bread to serve with dips or curries.

1 cup fine wholemeal plain flour

2 cups unbleached white flour

$^1/_2$ teaspoon vegetable salt

1 tablespoon butter or margarine

1 cup warm water

a little extra melted butter or margarine

Sift together the flours and salt. Rub the butter into the flour until it resembles breadcrumbs. Add the water all at once and using the hands mix to form a firm dough. Knead on a lightly floured board for 10 minutes. Divide the dough into 10 equal pieces and shape each into a smooth ball. Roll out each ball into a circle. Brush each with the melted shortening. Cut a slit from the centre to the edge and roll up as a cone shape, flatten the cone then roll it out again to a small plate size. Cook on both sides in a lightly oiled frypan until lightly golden. Serve warm.

PINEAPPLE COOLER

$^1/_2$ cup fresh pineapple juice

$^1/_2$ cup mineral water

$^1/_2$ banana

2 mint leaves

4 ice cubes

nutmeg

Blend all ingredients in a blender and serve dusted with nutmeg. Decorate the glass rim with a wedge of fresh pineapple.

SIMON'S SUPER BREAKFAST CEREAL

With a special thank you to my eldest nephew Simon, for his effort and enthusiasm in creating this great breakfast dish that is suitable for any hungry teenager.

'Breakfast is a time for fun,
the start of a new day.
Here's my super breakfast cereal,
to send you on your way'
— SIMON L DARCY

2 tablespoons of brown rice bubbles
1 tablespoon of toasted muesli
1 tablespoon of rolled oats
1 tablespoon of rice flakes
1 breakfast wheat biscuit
½ tablespoon of sultanas
1 sliced banana
soy milk (or cow's milk) as needed

Combine all of the dry ingredients, sultanas, and banana in a large breakfast bowl. Add the milk and there you go!

The combination of the grains used here — wheat, oats and rice — together with the soy milk gives a very nutritious and well balanced complex carbohydrate and protein combination. It provides a great start to the day.

SPRING ROLL PASTRY

1 cup finely ground wholemeal flour
1 cup unbleached white flour
¾-1 cup water
1 teaspoon oil

Sift the flours together. Add the water and oil to mix to a stiff dough. Roll the dough out on a well floured board until it is paper thin. With a sharp knife, trim edges to form a square and then cut into approximately 16 cm squares. Cover the squares with a slightly damp cloth or dust each with flour and stack until ready to use.

TAMATAR CHATNI

A tasty and popular tomato chutney from India.

1 kg tomatoes
2 onions, finely chopped
2 teaspoons finely chopped fresh root ginger
1 cup each chopped dates, raisins and currants
1 teaspoon chilli powder
2 teaspoons tamari
½ tablespoon oil
2 teaspoons mustard seeds

The tomatoes need to be peeled and this can be done after either holding them on a fork, over a flame for a brief time, or by popping them for only a few seconds in a saucepan of boiling water. Chop the peeled tomatoes. Place all of the ingredients, except the oil and mustard seeds, in a saucepan and bring to the boil, stirring occasionally. Reduce the heat and simmer uncovered for 1½ to 2 hours or until the chutney is thick. Meanwhile, heat the oil in a small frypan. Add the mustard seeds and fry for a couple of minutes until they stop popping. Add the mustard seeds to the chutney and stir well.

Serve hot or cold with vegetable loaves, patties, or pies. Refrigerate to store any left over. A teaspoon of dissolved kuzu or cornflower can be stirred in just prior to the end of cooking time to thicken the chutney.

Glossary

AGAR-AGAR
is a sea vegetable that acts as a jelling agent. It has properties similar to gelatine in that it can be dissolved in liquid, mixed with other ingredients, and when cooled will set like a jelly. Agar-agar, which is preferred by vegetarians, is easier to use than gelatine, which is an animal product. Any recipe using gelatine can be converted to use agar-agar using the same quantity of agar-agar powder, and twice as much if you are using agar-agar flakes. Agar-agar can be used to set moulded jellies, desserts, cheesecakes, fruit jellies, jam and icecream.

ARROWROOT
a fine starchy powder from the root of the arrowroot plant. It is used as a binder or thickener, or as a glaze over fruit pies.

BUCKWHEAT FLOUR
is made from ground buckwheat kernels. It has a slightly bitter flavour and is suitable for people who cannot tolerate wheat or gluten. Buckwheat is high in some of the minerals which are important for our nervous system.

CAROB
with a flavour similar to chocolate, carob powder is made from the ground carob bean, and is far healthier than chocolate. Carob does not contain the stimulants oxalic acid, caffeine or theobromine that chocolate contains and which speed up the heart beat and interfere with calcium absorption. The age old remedy of warm milk and cocoa before bed so that the calcium can relax the nervous system and give a good night's sleep in fact does the exact opposite.

Carob powder is richer and heavier than cocoa so less can be used when substituting for cocoa in recipes. Carob powder can be used in cakes, cookies, desserts, drinks and icings. Carob blocks and bars tend to have a high sugar content, however unsweetened carob products are available and can be a delight.

CREAMED COCONUT
can be used in curries, desserts, drinks etc, as a thick and creamy milk. Coconut is not a high protein food as other nuts are and as it is high in cholesterol its use needs to be limited.

COLD PRESSED OIL
is oil that is extracted from seeds, beans or nuts without the use of heat. It is believed that extracting the oil with heat destroys some of the vitamin content, and that carcinogenic products can develop. A small amount of oil in our diet is important as oil supplies unsaturated fatty acids which transport some essential vitamins around our body. As there is conflicting advice on the best oils to

use, the safest bet is to use small amounts of cold pressed oils and buy oil in glass or tin containers as foods stored for long terms in plastics can be damaging to our health.

KUZU
is a Japanese arrowoot, which although a little expensive, is lovely to cook with. It is similar to cornflour and arrowroot and is used as a thickener for sauces, jams, pies, syrups etc. Kuzu is also known for its medicinal value.

MAPLE SYRUP
is the natural sap from the Canadian maple tree and can be used for sweetening in place of honey or sugar. Make sure you obtain pure maple syrup as it can often contain extra sugar and colouring.

MISO
is a paste made from fermented soybeans. Miso is a good source of vitamins particularly B12 and minerals in a readily digestable form and adds a delightful richness to foods. There are various types of miso depending on the grains combined with soybeans, for example rice, wheat, or buckwheat. Miso is a concentrated food and keeps well. It has a salt content so needs to be used with discretion in low salt diets. Miso is added late in the cooking for soups, casseroles, sauces etc, as prolonged cooking tends to alter the digestive enzymes.

OATS
are an excellent grain and are a good source of protein, iron, calcium, B complex vitamins, and fats. Although traditionally a breakfast food, oats can be combined with wheat flour or other grains to make breads, pastries, pie crusts, cookies, cakes and pancakes.

RICOTTA CHEESE
is a delicious fresh Italian curd cheese, similar to cottage cheese, and has a very pleasant nut-like sweet flavour. Ricotta is rich in protein and minerals and lends itself perfectly to sweet dishes, cakes, mousses etc, as well as savoury nut loaves, dips, vegetable stuffings, salads, filo-pastry dishes etc. Ricotta is low in kilojoules, yet high in protein.

SHOYU
is a good quality soy sauce that is made from a mixture of fermented soybeans and wheat. Shoyu, which is a little milder than tamari, adds a rich flavour to foods and is available in a low-salt variety.

SOY MILK
is often used by people who are allergic to cow's milk and is the milk made from cooked and pressed soybeans. Soy milk provides protein and some B vitamins, but lacks the calcium that is in cow's milk, so this would need to be provided elsewhere in the diet if soy milk was being used as a substitute for cow's milk.

Natural soy milk can be used in place of cow's milk in recipes, but as it is rather expensive it can be diluted a little with water. There are a wide range of soy milks available on the market, some delightfully flavoured. However read the ingredients carefully as many have a form of sugar such as lactose, maltose, etc added.

SPROUTS
Vitality in foods is one of the most important factors in health, and this is exactly what sprouts offer. Because they are sprouted from seeds or beans and are actually still growing, they are rich in vitamins and minerals at their peak of nutrition. Sprouts also supply protein and can be quickly and conveniently grown in small areas.

SUGARLESS JAM
or natural jam is made without the addition of refined sugar, or chemical sugar substitutes. The jams are made with fruit and dried fruits and are thickened with pectin, kuzu, or arrowroot. Sugarless jams are delicious and so rich that only small amounts need to be used.

TAHINI
is a delightful paste made from ground sesame seeds and is used as a thickening binding and flavouring agent. Tahini is a Middle Eastern food and is rich in the minerals, calcium, magnesium, phosphorus and iron. Calcium is a mineral that is difficult to obtain in a dairy free diet, so tahini can be a good source of calcium.

However, as tahini is a fairly oily and concentrated food product it is a good idea to blend it with a little lemon juice or water. Tahini makes delicious spreads for sandwiches, salad dressings, sauces and dips. It can also be added to pies, casseroles, cakes, cheesecakes, puddings and biscuits. Although tahini can become addictive and can dominate in flavour its use is endless and is well worth experimenting with.

TAMARI
is a pure, good quality soy sauce with a rich natural flavour and is made from soybeans, water and salt. Low-salt tamari is available. Tamari is free from chemicals and preservatives, and has no colouring or artificial ingredients added. Tamari is used as a flavouring agent and takes the place of added salt or stock cubes in soups, vegetable dishes, pies, casseroles, dressings etc. It imparts a rich, full and pleasant flavour which blends easily with the foods. Tamari is certainly an important food to use in vegetarian dishes.

TEMPEH
is another soybean food and is made from cooked soybeans that are held together by a mould culture, and set in a flat cake. Tempeh is low in fat, low in carbohydrates, high in protein, digestive enzymes, and fibre. Tempeh also contains vitamin B12 which is difficult to obtain in a meat free diet. Tempeh will keep a week refrigerated and should have a fresh nutty smell. It can be successfully frozen. As it has a strong distinctive flavour and chewy texture, tempeh can be stir fried and used for kebabs, burgers,

pizzas, or added hot to salads, casseroles or soups at the last minute. Tempeh is just perfect for vegetarians at a barbecue as slabs of it can be cooked on a hot plate and eaten as a hamburger with salads or in buns with a good tomato sauce.

TOFU

or bean curd is a white custard-like substance made from set soy bean milk. Tofu is a high protein, low fat, low kilojoule, low carbohydrate, and cholesterol free food. Tofu is easy to digest and is an excellent food particularly for those cutting down on animal products in their diet and for children and babies. The most common form of tofu available is a largish square block which needs to be refrigerated and will keep about 5 days in water if it is changed regularly.

When tofu gets a little old it develops a yellow slimy surface which needs to be sliced off. Tofu can be frozen, however it has a tougher spongy texture when thawed. It can then be used in casseroles, soups or loaves where a chewy texture is desired. Tofu is an extremely interesting food to use as its bland flavour makes it very versatile. Because of its smooth texture tofu can be sliced, diced, mashed or blended to a cream, and it can be tossed in soups, marinated in salads, made into dips and spreads, added to loaves, vegie burgers, hot vegetable dishes, pasta dishes, or used in desserts, cakes, cheesecakes, or icecream.

Tofu needs very little cooking, basically just heating through.

Index

HOT VEGETABLE DISHES AND MAIN COURSES

DESSERTS

DRESSINGS, SAUCES AND SPREADS

CAKES AND COOKIES

ALSO ...